JUICING FOR BEGINNERS

Unlock Natural Wellness with Tasty and Effective Basic Recipes for Your Health.

30-DAY Meel Plan to Lose Weight

SKYE ADKINS

Table of Contents

INTRODUCTION

Welcome to the vibrant world of juicing! If you've picked up this book, you're likely curious about juicing or ready to dive into this nourishing practice. Perhaps you've heard of the myriad health benefits of fresh juices or been inspired by stories of those who've transformed their health through the magic of liquid greens and fruits. Whatever your motivation, you're on the brink of a transformative journey that revitalizes your body and invigorates your soul.

As some might believe, juicing isn't merely a trend or a shortcut to weight loss. Various cultures have embraced an ancient practice for its holistic benefits. It's about connecting with nature's pure essence, capturing the vitality of fruits and vegetables, and delivering this life force directly to our cells.

In "Juicing for Beginners," we'll unravel the complexities, in both a literal and metaphorical sense, as we journey through the universe of juices. From grasping the principles underpinning juicing and its impact on our well-being to navigating the extensive selection of ingredients and recipes that can elevate your concoctions, this book serves as your all-encompassing manual.

Whether you're a health enthusiast looking to add another layer to your wellness routine, a busy individual seeking quick nutrient-packed solutions, or someone dealing with health issues hoping to find natural ways to boost healing—there's something here for you.

If you are new to juicing, talking to your doctor before starting a juicing regimen is a good idea. It's essential if you have any underlying health conditions.

So, ready your juicers and open your minds as we embark on this journey together.

WHAT IS JUICING?

Embarking on the juicing travel requires a foundational understanding of the process and its significance in nutrition. For newcomers to this vibrant practice, let's delve into the juicing essentials, setting the stage for an informed and enriching experience.

Defining Juicing: At its core, juicing is extracting the liquid from fresh fruits and vegetables. This extracted liquid is a concentrated source of vitamins, minerals, antioxidants, and other beneficial compounds in the produce.

The Equipment: While various purification methods exist, most individuals rely on juicers. Specially designed appliances separate the juice from the fibrous pulp. There are mainly two types of juicers: centrifugal (which extracts juice by spinning at high speeds) and masticating (which crushes and presses the produce to extract juice). Each has its advantages and specific use cases.

Whole Foods vs. Juice: Juicing removes most of the fiber in whole fruits and vegetables. The resultant liquid is smoother, easier to consume, and more rapidly absorbed by the body. While entire foods have benefits, including promoting digestive health, juicing offers unique advantages, especially in concentrated nutrient intake.

The Art of Combining: Juicing isn't just about extracting liquid from a single fruit or vegetable. For many, it's an art form combining various produce types to achieve a desired flavor profile or nutritional goal. The combinations are endless, from sweet fruit concoctions to green vegetable elixirs, catering to every palate and purpose.

Nutritional Density: Because juicing allows for the consumption of a larger volume of produce in liquid form, it can be a way to boost one's intake of essential nutrients. For instance, someone might find it challenging to eat six whole carrots, but juicing them allows them to consume the nutrient content in a single glass.

Purity and Freshness: One of the primary appeals of juicing is the ability to control the ingredients. Unlike store-bought juices, which may contain additives, preservatives, or excessive sugars, homemade juices are fresh, pure, and free from unwanted additives.

Aids in Hydration: Beyond just nutrients, the high water content in many fruits and vegetables contributes to hydration. Fresh juices can be a flavorful way to contribute to daily hydration needs.

A Gateway to Better Nutrition: For many, juicing is a stepping stone to embracing a more health-conscious lifestyle. The ease of consuming nutrients and the delightful flavors can motivate individuals to incorporate more fresh produce into their diets, whether in liquid or solid form.

In summation, juicing is a dynamic practice that transforms fresh produce into nutrient-dense beverages. While it doesn't replace the need for whole fruits and vegetables in a diet, it complements them, offering a unique and delicious way to bolster one's nutritional intake. As we journey further into this book, we'll explore the myriad facets of juicing, from techniques and recipes to its profound health implications.

JUICE-MAKING EQUIPMENT

Stepping into the juicing world can be exciting and overwhelming, especially when selecting the right equipment. Like any culinary endeavor, the tools you choose can significantly impact the quality of your end product. Here, we'll demystify the key equipment options available, their features, and how to choose the best fit for your juicing journey.

ESSENTIAL EQUIPMENT: JUICERS

When we talk about juice-making equipment, the first thing that comes to mind is the juicer. Here are the primary types:

Centrifugal Juicers:
Function: Uses a high-speed spinning action to extract juice.
Pros: Quick, affordable, and easy to find.
Cons: It can be noisy, less efficient at extracting juice (especially from leafy greens), and may produce more heat, which can reduce the nutrient content.

Masticating Juicers (Cold Press or Slow Juicers):
Function: Crushes and presses fruits and vegetables at a slower speed.
Pros: More efficient juice extraction, retains more nutrients, and can handle leafy greens and wheatgrass effectively.
Cons: Typically more expensive and can be slower in processing.

Twin-Gear (Triturating) Juicers:
Function: Uses two rotating gears to crush and grind produce.
Pros: Offers the highest yield, especially for leafy greens and wheatgrass, and retains maximum nutrients.
Cons: Often the most expensive and requires more preparation time.

Manual or Hand Press Juicers:
Function: Operated by hand, often using a press mechanism.
Pros: Portable, doesn't require electricity, and often affordable.
Cons: Suitable mainly for citrus fruits and can be labor-intensive.

OTHER HELPFUL ACCESSORIES:

While the juicer is the main star, other tools can enhance your juice-making experience:

1. Produce Cleaner Brush: This small tool helps scrub the dirt off fruits and vegetables, ensuring they're clean before juicing.

2. Sharp Knife and Chopping Board: Essential for prepping your fruits and veggies, especially for masticating and triturating juicers.
3. Fine Mesh Strainer: A filter can be handy if you prefer juice without pulp or foam.
4. Glass or Stainless Steel Containers: For storing any leftover juice. These materials don't leach unwanted chemicals and help retain the juice's freshness.
5. Reusable Produce Bags: Environmentally friendly and handy for shopping and storing your fresh produce.
6. Citrus Press: If you consume a lot of citrus-based juices, a dedicated citrus press can be more efficient than a standard juicer.
7. Vegetable Wash or Spray: To help remove pesticides and contaminants from non-organic produce.
8. Pulp Storage Containers: If you intend to save and repurpose the pulp for other recipes.
9. Blender: For those days, you might want a smoothie instead or to blend in softer fruits or add-ins like avocado.
10. Reusable Metal or Glass Straws: An eco-friendly option instead of disposable straws for juice.
11. Compost Bin: If you like to be eco-friendly, a compost bin is excellent for disposing of your fruit and vegetable waste.
12. Calendar or Journal: Track your juicing habits, jot down your favorite recipes, and note how different juices make you feel.

CONSIDERATIONS FOR CHOOSING THE RIGHT EQUIPMENT

When deciding on the right equipment, consider:
- **Budget:** How much are you willing to invest?
- **Type of Produce:** A masticating or twin-gear juicer might be better if you're juicing a lot of leafy greens.
- **Frequency of Use:** Investing in a more durable and efficient juicer might be worthwhile if you're juicing daily.
- **Storage Space:** Ensure you have enough space in your kitchen for the juicer and other equipment.
- **Ease of Cleaning:** Some juicers are more cumbersome to clean than others, which can be a significant factor for many.

Choosing the right juice-making equipment is crucial for a beginner. Your choice will set the tone for your juicing experience, impacting everything from the quality of your juice to the time you spend preparing and cleaning up. Remember to prioritize your needs and preferences, ensuring your equipment aligns with your juicing goals and lifestyle.

THE HEALTH BENEFITS OF JUICING

NUTRIENT BOOST

As beginners set foot into the world of juicing, one of the primary motivations is often the allure of a potent nutrient boost. With our modern diets usually falling short of recommended fruit and vegetable intakes, juicing can bridge that gap and ensure our bodies receive the necessary nourishment. This subchapter will explore why juicing acts as a veritable nutrient powerhouse:

- **Concentrated Goodness:** Juicing is akin to distilling the essence of fruits and vegetables. By removing most of the fibrous content, what remains is a liquid rich in vitamins, minerals, enzymes, and antioxidants. This means you could consume the nutritional equivalent of several servings of whole fruits and vegetables in just one glass.
- **Bioavailability**: A significant advantage of juicing is the enhanced bioavailability of certain nutrients. Without fiber slowing the digestive process, the body can absorb many nutrients in juice more rapidly and efficiently. This ensures that more of the ingested vitamins and minerals enter your system.
- **Phytonutrient Intake:** Plants contain compounds known as phytonutrients, beyond just vitamins and minerals. These substances, which give plants their color, flavor, and resistance to disease, have been shown to offer a range of health benefits for humans. Juicing provides an easy means to increase your intake of these valuable compounds.
- **Enzymatic Wealth:** Freshly pressed juices are replete with natural enzymes. Enzymes catalyze many of our body's chemical reactions, aiding digestion and nutrient absorption. Drinking juice immediately after making it ensures that these enzymes stay active and offer their full benefit.
- **Customization for Nutritional Needs:** One of the beauties of juicing is the ability to tailor your concoctions to your specific nutritional needs. Need more iron? Add some spinach or kale to your juice. Are you seeking a vitamin C boost? Incorporate citrus fruits. This flexibility allows you to address any dietary insufficiencies head-on.
- **Synergistic Effects:** By combining multiple fruits and vegetables in one juice, you benefit from individual nutrients and their synergistic effects. When consumed together, some compounds enhance each other's absorption and efficacy. For example, combining vitamin C-rich fruits with leafy greens can enhance iron absorption from the greens.

DIGESTIVE BENEFITS

Digestion is a complex yet crucial process that our bodies perform daily. Ensuring its optimal function affects nutrient absorption and our overall sense of well-being. While whole fruits and vegetables already play a pivotal role in promoting digestive health, their juiced counterparts offer unique benefits. This subchapter unveils the profound influence juicing can have on our digestive system:

- **Ease of Digestion:** Juices are relatively more accessible for the stomach and intestines to process without the bulk of insoluble fiber. This makes juicing especially beneficial for those with sensitive or compromised digestive systems. The nutrients in the juice are absorbed quickly, requiring less energy and effort from the digestive tract.
- **Soluble Fiber and Gut Health:** While juicing almost removes insoluble fiber, it retains a good amount of soluble fiber. This fiber dissolves in water and forms a gel-like substance in the gut, which can act as a prebiotic. Prebiotics feed beneficial gut bacteria, promoting a healthy microbiome integral to overall digestive health.
- **Natural Digestive Enzymes:** Certain fruits, like pineapple and papaya, are renowned for their digestive enzymes—bromelain and papain, respectively. Juicing preserves these enzymes, which aid in breaking down foods and absorbing nutrients, especially proteins.
- **Hydration for Digestion:** An often-underestimated component of good digestion is adequate hydration. Water is essential for many digestive processes, including the smooth movement of food through the intestines. Juicing, especially with high-water-content produce, contributes to the body's hydration, indirectly benefiting digestion.
- **Alleviation of Bloating and Indigestion:** Since juices are more easily digestible, they can alleviate symptoms like bloating or indigestion in some individuals. It's especially beneficial when one's system needs a break from heavy or hard-to-digest foods.
- **Nutrients for Gut-Lining Repair:** Juices, especially those made from leafy greens and cruciferous vegetables, contain essential nutrients and antioxidants that can help repair the gut lining. This is especially significant for individuals with conditions like leaky gut syndrome.
- **Balancing Stomach Acidity:** Some juices, such as cabbage juice, have been traditionally used to balance stomach acidity levels, which can benefit those with acid reflux or ulcers.
- **Aiding Liver Detoxification:** The liver plays a central role in digestion, particularly in bile production, which breaks down fats. When consumed in juiced form, certain compounds in fruits and vegetables can support liver function and detoxification processes, indirectly enhancing digestion.
- **Stimulating Appetite:** Sipping on a small amount of fresh juice can be an appetizer for those struggling with a reduced appetite. The flavors and nutrients can stimulate gastric juices, preparing the stomach for a meal.

DETOXIFICATION:

The concept of detoxification, often called a "detox", has grown in popularity in recent years. Detoxification involves removing harmful substances from the body and promoting overall wellness. Juicing is one of the most natural and refreshing ways to aid this process.

Before diving into how juicing aids detoxification, it's essential to understand what toxins are. Pollution, processed foods, pesticides, and other sources expose us to many toxins daily. Over time, these toxins can accumulate in our bodies, leading to various health issues such as fatigue, digestion problems, and even chronic diseases.

Benefits of Juicing for Detoxification:

- **Rich in Nutrients:** Juices are densely packed with essential vitamins and minerals. These nutrients nourish our cells and enhance our body's natural detoxifying systems, such as the liver, kidneys, and skin.
- **Hydration:** Proper hydration is crucial for detoxification. Fresh juices, rich in water content, ensure our cells stay well-hydrated, support kidney function, and efficiently remove metabolic waste.

- **Digestive Reset:** Juicing gives our digestive system a break since juices are more accessible to digest than solid foods. This allows the body to divert energy from digestion to detoxification and cellular repair.
- **Alkalizing Effect:** Many fresh juices, especially those made from green vegetables, have an alkalizing effect on the body. Toxins and harmful microorganisms are believed to increase less in an alkaline environment.
- **Digestive Rest:** Liquid nutrition, like juices, gives the digestive system a minor break, allowing the body to prioritize detoxification and cellular repair.
- **Phytonutrients:** Many plants contain phytonutrients, compounds that benefit our health. Some of these phytonutrients specifically assist our body's detox processes:
- **Glucosinolates** (found in cruciferous vegetables like broccoli, kale, and Brussels sprouts): These compounds support Phase II detoxification in the liver, assisting the body in neutralizing and removing toxins.
- **Quercetin** (found in apples and onions): This antioxidant supports the liver's detoxification pathway and has anti-inflammatory properties.

When juicing for detoxification, it's crucial to use organic produce to reduce the intake of additional pesticides and chemicals.

ENHANCED ENERGY LEVELS:

One of the commonly reported benefits of juicing is enhanced energy levels. Let's explore this topic in detail:

- **Direct Nutrient Channeling:** You drink a concentrated potion of vitamins, minerals, and enzymes when you consume juice. Without the bulk of insoluble fiber, these nutrients are rapidly assimilated into the bloodstream, ensuring quicker energy delivery.
- **Rich in B Vitamins:** Many fruits and vegetables, especially greens like spinach and kale, are rich in B vitamins. These vitamins play a crucial role in energy production at a cellular level. A deficiency in B vitamins can lead to fatigue.
- **The Hydration Boost:** With their high water content, juices provide a dual benefit of nutrients and hydration, ensuring that your cells function optimally and energy production remains unhampered.
- **Oxygen – The Silent Energizer:** Chlorophyll, abundant in green leafy veggies, has a structure similar to our red blood cells. This green pigment can support oxygen transport, and with better-oxygenated blood, you're looking at enhanced vitality and alertness.
- **Balancing Act – Alkalinity:** An over-acidic environment in the body can be a hidden energy thief. Many fresh juices have alkalizing effects, helping maintain a harmonious pH level, which can, in turn, promote better energy levels.
- **The Detox Connection:** While the word 'detox' is thrown around a lot, at its core, it's about reducing the burdens on our bodies. Juicing can aid in this by providing antioxidants and flushing out toxins, ensuring that our bodily processes, including energy production, run smoothly.

SUPPORTING IMMUNE FUNCTION:

Vitamins and minerals like vitamin C, beta-carotene, and zinc are crucial for a robust immune system. Regularly consuming juices rich in these nutrients can bolster your body's defenses against illnesses.

Here's how your freshly squeezed concoctions can act as allies for your immune system:

- **The Prowess of Vitamin C:** Fruits like oranges, lemons, and grapefruits are abundant in vitamin C. This antioxidant-rich vitamin is crucial for bolstering the immune system, facilitating several cellular processes that fend off invaders.
- **A Treasure Trove of Bioactive Elements:** Our favorite fruits and vegetables contain polyphenols, flavonoids, and carotenoids. Beyond their vibrant hues, these elements showcase anti-inflammatory and antioxidant capabilities, supporting the body's defenses.
- **The Marvel of Minerals:** Elements like zinc in leafy greens like spinach or selenium in specific seeds are vital for immune responses. Incorporating these into your juices can give your immunity an extra edge.
- **Immunity from the Gut:** Much of our immune activity is rooted in our digestive system. Ingredients like celery or papaya can foster a beneficial gut environment, indirectly nurturing a resilient immune response.
- **The Allium Advantage:** Garlic and onions, members of the allium family, contain allicin. This unique compound has been studied for its potential to act against microbes, enhancing our natural defenses.

WEIGHT MANAGEMENT:

When approached mindfully, Juicing can be a powerful weight management tool. It allows the body to receive a high concentration of beneficial nutrients, antioxidants, and enzymes without the added calories from solid foods. This subchapter will delve into the benefits and considerations of using juicing for weight management and provide practical tips to integrate it into your daily routine.

Juicing can play a supportive role in weight management in several ways:

- **Satiety and Nutrient Intake:** Freshly pressed juices provide a concentrated source of vitamins, minerals, and antioxidants. These nutrients can help maintain energy levels and reduce cravings for unhealthy foods.
- **Low-Calorie Refreshment:** If crafted correctly, juices can be a refreshing, lower-calorie alternative to high-calorie beverages and snacks.

Making the Right Juice Choices:

- **Greens are Gold:** Leafy greens like spinach, kale, and chard are low in calories and nutrients. They can be the primary base for many weight management-focused juices.
- **Limit Sugary Fruits:** While fruits like mangoes, bananas, and grapes are nutritious, they are also high in sugars. Opt for lower-sugar fruits like berries, green apples, or kiwi when juicing for weight control.
- **Prioritize Vegetables:** While fruits are a delicious and nutritious juicing component, they also come with natural sugars. Make vegetables the primary ingredients in your juices to keep the calorie and sugar content in check. Green leafy veggies like spinach, kale, and cucumbers are excellent choices.
- **Add Protein:** Add natural protein sources like chia or spirulina to your juices. Protein can help you feel full, aiding in weight management.
- **Limit High-Calorie Ingredients:** Ingredients like avocados and nuts, while super nutritious, are also calorie-dense. It's essential to use these sparingly if weight management is your goal.

What Juicing Can't Do:

- **Replace All Meals:** Juices can be a supplementary nutrition source but should only replace some meals. Solid foods contain fibers, proteins, and fats crucial for satiety and overall health.
- **Miracle Weight Loss:** No single food or juice recipe can magically melt away pounds. Weight management through juicing should be a part of a comprehensive strategy that includes a balanced diet and regular physical activity.

Tips to Incorporate Juicing for Weight Management:

- **Start Small:** If you're new to juicing, begin with more straightforward recipes with a mix of fruits and veggies. As your palate becomes more accustomed, gradually increase the vegetable content.
- **Stay Mindful of Portions:** Portion control is vital even with juices. Aim for servings of 8-16 ounces (240-480 milliliters) as a general guide.
- **Incorporate Fiber:** One of the drawbacks of juicing is the removal of fiber. Consider blending a portion of the pulp back into the juice or adding a tablespoon of chia or flaxseeds to boost fiber content.
- **Stay Hydrated:** While juicing, drink plenty of water. This not only supports metabolism but also aids in digestion.

Pair your juicing routine with other healthful habits:

- **Balanced Diet:** Ensure the rest of your meals are balanced with whole grains, lean proteins, healthy fats, and plenty of whole fruits and vegetables.
- **Regular Exercise:** Pairing your juicing regimen with consistent physical activity can aid in achieving your weight management goals more effectively.

In essence, juicing can be a delightful and nutritious addition to a beginner's journey into weight management. Proper knowledge, mindful choices, and a holistic approach can be valuable in your wellness toolkit. Juicing is more than a fleeting trend; it's a pathway to robust health, diverse flavors, and a deep appreciation for the natural wealth of fruits and vegetables.

SELECTING THE RIGHT INGREDIENTS

UNDERSTANDING THE BASICS

Juicing is a captivating journey into flavors, colors, and vibrant health. Before you embark on this exploration, it's pivotal to grasp the fundamentals of ingredient selection. This subchapter will simplify the process so you will understand the principle of making juices that are both delightful to the palate and beneficial for the body.

1. **The Nutritional Lens:** Every fruit or vegetable brings its unique nutrient profile. Think of vitamins, minerals, enzymes, and antioxidants. When selecting ingredients, consider what nutritional benefits you want to achieve.
2. **Sweetness Balance:** Fruits are nature's candies, full of natural sugars. While they offer delightful flavors, you'd want to strike a balance with vegetables to avoid excessive sugar intake. Greens like spinach or kale can balance out the sweetness of fruits like apples or pineapples.
3. **The Power of Greens:** Leafy greens are nutrient powerhouses. They may not always taste sweet or zesty, but their health benefits are remarkable. Rotating your greens (e.g., switching between kale, spinach, and romaine) can also give you a broader spectrum of nutrients.
4. **Texture Matters:** Every ingredient will influence the texture of your juice. While watermelon and cucumber are hydrating and yield a watery juice, avocados, and bananas give a creamy texture. Understanding this helps in achieving your preferred juice consistency.
5. **Color Palette:** Nature offers fruits and veggies in various colors. The rule of thumb is the broader the color spectrum in your glass, the more comprehensive the range of nutrients. Aim for a rainbow!
6. **Freshness is Key:** The fresher the produce, the better the taste, and the higher the nutrient content.
7. **To Peel or Not to Peel:** While many fruits and veggies are juiced with their skin on for added nutrients, some (like citrus fruits) might need peeling. If you're unsure about the pesticide residue, peel or opt for organic produce.
8. **Organic vs. Conventional:** While organic produce is free from synthetic pesticides, it can be pricier. If budget is a concern, consider the "Dirty Dozen" and "Clean Fifteen" lists to prioritize which items to buy organic.
9. **Explore Beyond Fruits and Veggies:** Don't restrict juicing to fruits and vegetables. Herbs like mint, parsley, or cilantro and spices like ginger or turmeric can add an exciting twist to your juices while amplifying the health benefits.
10. **Seasonal and Local Produce:** Seasonal fruits and vegetables taste better and are typically more nutrient-dense and environmentally friendly. Shopping locally can also introduce you to varieties you might not find in larger grocery chains.
11. **Clean Your Produce:** Always wash your produce to remove any dirt or lingering pesticides, even if you buy organic. A simple wash in a solution of vinegar and water can be effective.
12. **Listening to Your Body:** Everyone's body is different. What works for one might not work for another. Paying attention to how your body reacts to certain ingredients is essential. The beet gives you a rush of energy, or too much kale feels heavy. Adjust based on how you feel.

ESSENTIAL FRUITS FOR JUICING

People have juiced fruits for centuries because of their delicious taste, refreshing nature, and nutritional benefits. Here are some of the most essential fruits for juicing, each bringing its unique flavor profile and health benefits:

Apples
Nutritional Highlights: Apples are a great source of vitamin C, potassium, and phytonutrients source. They also contain soluble fiber, though the pulp holds most of it.
Taste Profile: They offer a balanced sweetness with a hint of tartness, making them versatile for many juice blends.
Juicing Tip: Choose organic apples to avoid pesticides and consider juicing them with the skin on to maximize nutrients.

Citrus Fruits (Oranges, Lemons, Limes, Grapefruits)
Nutritional Highlights: Packed with vitamin C, citrus fruits also provide potassium, folate, and various antioxidants.
Taste Profile: They range from sweet (oranges) to sour (lemons and limes) and can add a refreshing zest to your juices.
Juicing Tip: Peel off the outer skin, but try to retain as much white pith as possible - it's rich in beneficial flavonoids.

Berries (Strawberries, Blueberries, Raspberries)
Nutritional Highlights: Berries are antioxidant powerhouses, with vitamins C and K, manganese, and several phytonutrients.
Taste Profile: Their flavor ranges from sweet (strawberries) to tangy (raspberries), offering a delightful depth to juices.
Juicing Tip: Since berries can be soft, it's best to alternate juicing them with firmer fruits like apples to ensure maximum juice extraction.

Pineapple
Nutritional Highlights: It contains bromelain, an enzyme known for its digestive benefits, and is rich in vitamin C, manganese, and thiamine.
Taste Profile: Pineapples provide a tropical sweetness with a zesty undertone.
Juicing Tip: Remove the tough outer skin before juicing, but you can juice the core - it has a concentrated amount of bromelain.

Mango
Nutritional Highlights: Rich in vitamins A, C, and E, providing ample dietary fiber and antioxidants.
Taste Profile: Offers a creamy, tropical sweetness that can elevate the texture and flavor of your juice.
Juicing Tip: Mangoes can be pulpy, so blend the extracted juice for a smoother consistency.

Grapes
Nutritional Highlights: Provides vitamins C and K and powerful antioxidants like resveratrol.
Taste Profile: Grapes lend a subtle, sweet flavor, with red and purple grapes adding a touch of tartness.
Juicing Tip: Juice them whole, including the seeds, if they have any, as they contain beneficial oils and antioxidants.

Melons (Watermelon, Cantaloupe, Honeydew)
Nutritional Highlights: High in hydration, melons also offer vitamins A and C and potassium.
Taste Profile: They have a watery and mildly sweet flavor, making them a refreshing base for summer juices.

Juicing Tip: Juicing watermelon, including some of the rind, can boost the nutritional content, as it contains additional health compounds.

Once you've become familiar with the primary fruits for juicing, you might be eager to experiment and diversify your juice blends. The world of fruits offers abundant flavors, textures, and nutritional benefits. Here are some additional fruits to consider:

Peaches and Nectarines
Nutritional Highlights: Both fruits are rich in vitamins A, C, E, and K, as well as fiber and potassium.
Taste Profile: They impart a juicy, aromatic sweetness with a soft texture, enhancing the flavor depth of juices.
Juicing Tip: Ensure they're ripe for the best flavor and juice yield. Remember to remove the pits before juicing.

Cherries
Nutritional Highlights: Cherries are rich in vitamins C, A, and potassium and contain potent antioxidants, including anthocyanins.
Taste Profile: Providing a delightful balance of sweet and tart, cherries can enhance fruit and vegetable juice blends.
Juicing Tip: Always pit cherries before juicing to prevent any machine damage.

Passion Fruit
Nutritional Highlights: A rich source of vitamin C, dietary fiber, and beneficial plant compounds.
Taste Profile: Its intense tropical flavor can add an aromatic zing to any juice blend.
Juicing Tip: While the seeds are edible, you should strain them out for a smoother juice consistency.

Papaya
Nutritional Highlights: Contains an enzyme called papain, beneficial for digestion. It's also rich in vitamin C, folate, and potassium.
Taste Profile: Mildly sweet with buttery undertones, papayas can add a tropical note to juices.
Juicing Tip: Remove seeds before juicing, as they can impart a peppery taste.

Guava
Nutritional Highlights: Extremely rich in vitamin C, it also offers vitamin A, folic acid, and dietary fiber.
Taste Profile: With a unique combination of sweetness and acidity, guavas provide a tropical flair to juices.
Juicing Tip: Since guavas can be seedy, consider straining your juice after extraction.

Blackberries
Nutritional Highlights: Packed with vitamins C and K, fiber, and antioxidants.
Taste Profile: Their tangy-sweet flavor adds a rich depth and color to juice blends.
Juicing Tip: Blackberries are soft, so alternate with more complex fruits like apples for better extraction.

Plums
Nutritional Highlights: Contains vitamins A, C, K, and B, dietary fiber, and antioxidants.
Taste Profile: Sweet with a hint of tartness, plums can be a refreshing addition to juices.
Juicing Tip: Ensure they're pitted before juicing, and use ripe plums for maximum yield.

Figs
Nutritional Highlights: High in dietary fiber, calcium, magnesium, and potassium.
Taste Profile: Naturally sweet with a slightly jammy texture.
Juicing Tip: Since figs are very soft, they're best blended after other main juice ingredients and then mixed in.

Apricots
Nutritional Highlights: Offer vitamins A, C, and E, fiber, and potassium.
Taste Profile: Mildly sweet with a touch of tartness.
Juicing Tip: Remove the pits before juicing, and use ripe apricots for the best flavor.

One of the joys of juicing is discovering combinations that taste great and amplify each ingredient's health benefits. For instance, the vitamin C in citrus fruits can enhance iron absorption from leafy greens. As a beginner, don't hesitate to experiment and find blends that appeal to your taste and nutritional needs.

ESSENTIAL VEGETABLES FOR JUICING

When starting your juicing, the vast array of vegetables available might seem overwhelming. However, not all vegetables are equal regarding nutritional value, taste, and juicing efficiency. To help you wade through the choices, we've compiled a list of essential vegetables that are rich in nutrients and versatile for various juice recipes. Incorporating these veggies into your diet can be a game-changer for your health.

Kale
Nutritional Highlights: Kale is a powerhouse of vitamins A, K, and C. It also contains calcium, potassium, and a healthy dose of antioxidants.
Taste Profile: Earthy and slightly bitter.
Juicing Tip: Combining kale with fruits like apple or pineapple can help mask its bitterness.

Spinach
Nutritional Highlights: Loaded with iron, vitamin K, vitamin A, and folate.
Taste Profile: Mild and slightly sweet.
Juicing Tip: Spinach pairs well with almost any fruit or vegetable, making it an ideal base for many juice recipes.

Celery
Nutritional Highlights: Rich in vitamins A, K, and C, providing a good amount of fiber.
Taste Profile: Crisp with a hint of pepperiness.
Juicing Tip: Celery adds a refreshing taste and can dilute more robust flavors in your juice.

Carrots
Nutritional Highlights: Brimming with vitamin A in the form of beta-carotene is beneficial for eye health.
Taste Profile: Sweet and earthy.
Juicing Tip: Carrot juice provides a sweet base that pairs well with both fruits and vegetables.

Beets
Nutritional Highlights: Good source of folate, manganese, and potassium.
Taste Profile: Sweet and earthy with a hint of mineral-like flavor.
Juicing Tip: Beets can stain, so handle with care. Pairing beets with citrus fruits can create a delightful taste combination.

Cucumber
Nutritional Highlights: Contains vitamins K and C and is especially hydrating due to its high water content.

Taste Profile: Mild and refreshing.
Juicing Tip: Cucumber can add volume to your juice and balance out more robust flavors.

Ginger
Nutritional Highlights: Gingerol, the main bioactive compound in ginger, has powerful anti-inflammatory and antioxidant properties.
Taste Profile: Spicy and warming.
Juicing Tip: Use ginger sparingly, as its strong flavor can dominate. It pairs well with citrus fruits and adds a zing to your juice.

Broccoli
Nutritional Highlights: Packed with vitamins C, K, and A, as well as folate.
Taste Profile: Green and slightly bitter.
Juicing Tip: Broccoli stems juice well and have a milder flavor than the florets.

Wheatgrass
Nutritional Highlights: Contains chlorophyll, vitamins A, C, and E, and amino acids.
Taste Profile: Very green with a slight sweetness.
Juicing Tip: A little goes a long way. Start with a small amount and gradually increase.

Sweet Potatoes
Nutritional Highlights: Rich in beta-carotene, vitamin C, and potassium.
Taste Profile: Sweet and creamy.
Juicing Tip: Mix with apple or pineapple for a sweet, dessert-like juice.

Tomatoes
Nutritional Highlights: Tomatoes are a rich source of vitamins A, C, and K. They also contain significant amounts of potassium, folate, and thiamine. One of the standout compounds in tomatoes is lycopene, a powerful antioxidant known for its potential protective effects against certain types of cancers, particularly prostate cancer. Moreover, tomatoes have other beneficial plant compounds like beta-carotene, naringenin, and chlorogenic acid.
Taste Profile: Tomatoes offer a savory, tangy flavor with a hint of sweetness. Their taste can vary based on their ripeness and variety, with some being exceptionally sweet and others more acidic.
Juicing Tip: Using ripe, juicy tomatoes for juicing is preferable. While many choose to remove the seeds for smoother juice, you can include them since they have additional nutrients. When juicing tomatoes, pair them with other savory vegetables like celery or bell peppers, or add a dash of salt or herbs to enhance their natural flavor. Given the watery nature of tomatoes, they often produce a good amount of juice.

Swiss Chard
Nutritional Highlights: Offers a rich supply of vitamins A, K, and C, along with magnesium and potassium.
Taste Profile: Slightly earthy with a hint of bitterness.
Juicing Tip: Pairs well with cucumber or apple to balance its more robust flavor.

Fennel
Nutritional Highlights: Contains vitamin C, potassium, and a unique array of antioxidants.
Taste Profile: Anise-like flavor with a hint of sweetness.
Juicing Tip: Fennel can be dominant, so it's best to use it sparingly and mix it with milder flavors.

Parsley
Nutritional Highlights: Rich in vitamins K, C, and A, and a good source of folate.
Taste Profile: Fresh and slightly peppery.
Juicing Tip: Add parsley for a vibrant color and to introduce a fresh kick.

Zucchini
Nutritional Highlights: Contains B vitamins, potassium, and vitamin C.
Taste Profile: Mild and slightly sweet.
Juicing Tip: Great for adding volume without introducing a strong flavor, making it versatile for many recipes.

Bell Peppers
Nutritional Highlights: An excellent source of vitamin C, vitamin B6, and folate.
Taste Profile: Sweet and crisp.
Juicing Tip: Red bell peppers are sweeter than green, adding a lovely color to your juice.

Cabbage
Nutritional Highlights: Packed with vitamins C and K and essential minerals.
Taste Profile: Mild with a subtle sweetness.
Juicing Tip: Combining cabbage with apple or carrot can produce a pleasant and balanced juice.

Romaine Lettuce
Nutritional Highlights: Provides vitamins A, K, and C and is a good folate source.
Taste Profile: Mild and slightly watery.
Juicing Tip: Romaine is an excellent base for juices due to its neutral flavor.

Bok Choy
Nutritional Highlights: Contains vitamins A, C, and K, calcium, and other minerals.
Taste Profile: Mildly peppery with a hint of mustard
Juicing Tip: Its stems are crunchy and hold much water

Garlic
Nutritional Highlights: Garlic contains abundant manganese, vitamins B6 and C, and selenium. It's also rich in bioactive compounds such as allicin, which have powerful health effects.
Taste Profile: Strong, savory, and spicy when raw, which mellows and sweetens when roasted or cooked.
Juicing Tip: Given its potent flavor, a small clove of garlic can infuse its taste into a large batch of juice. It pairs well with tomato-based juices and can provide a savory kick. Always be cautious with the quantity, as its taste can dominate.

Onions
Nutritional Highlights: Onions are rich in vitamins C and B6, folate, and potassium. They also contain many antioxidants and compounds like quercetin that offer anti-inflammatory benefits.
Taste Profile: Sharp and spicy when raw, they sweeten considerably when cooked. The intensity and sweetness can vary depending on the variety (red, white, yellow, or green).
Juicing Tip: While not common in fruit juices, onions can be a unique addition to vegetable-based juices, especially those with a savory profile. Use milder onion varieties, like green onions or shallots, to avoid overpowering the juice. As with garlic, it's crucial to use onions sparingly.

The world of vegetable juicing is vast, but starting with these essential vegetables can ensure you get diverse nutrients. As you become more experienced, you can experiment with different combinations but remember to always listen to your body and adjust your juice ingredients accordingly.

BOOSTERS & SUPERFOODS IN JUICING

When crafting the perfect juice, the devil is often in the details. Beyond standard fruits and vegetables, you can add several boosters and enhancers to improve your drink's flavor and nutritional value. Here's a breakdown of some of the most popular options:

Chia Seeds
Nutritional Highlights: A significant source of omega-3 fatty acids, these seeds also provide ample fiber, protein, and antioxidants.
Taste Profile: Mild and neutral, offering a slightly nutty undertone.
Juicing Tip: Due to their ability to absorb water, chia seeds can add a gelatinous texture to your juice. It's best to sprinkle them in post-juicing for a texture boost.

Flax Seeds
Nutritional Highlights: Loaded with heart-healthy omega-3 fats, they also offer beneficial lignans and fiber.
Taste Profile: Mildly nutty and earthy.
Juicing Tip: Opt for ground flax seeds over whole ones to unleash their nutritional potential. This ensures better absorption.

Mint
Nutritional Highlights: Mint is refreshing, has digestive benefits, and is rich in vitamins like vitamin A.
Taste Profile: Cool and crisp, offering a refreshing touch.
Juicing Tip: A few leaves go a long way; add incrementally to avoid overpowering your juice.

Turmeric
Nutritional Highlights: A potent anti-inflammatory ingredient, it's rich in curcumin, a powerful antioxidant.
Taste Profile: Earthy with a hint of pepperiness.
Juicing Tip: Combine with a pinch of black pepper to enhance the absorption of curcumin.

Wheatgrass
Nutritional Highlights: Highly alkalizing and filled with chlorophyll, amino acids, vitamins, and enzymes.
Taste Profile: Fresh, grassy, and slightly bitter.
Juicing Tip: If you're juicing wheatgrass at home, ensure it's finely chopped to extract maximum juice. You should consume it in moderation because of its strong flavor.

Moringa
Nutritional Highlights: Dubbed the "drumstick tree," moringa is rich in vitamins, minerals, and amino acids.
Taste Profile: Earthy with a hint of bitterness.

Juicing Tip: As with most potent ingredients, start with a smaller amount and adjust based on your palate. It pairs well with sweet fruits like pineapples or mangoes to counteract bitterness.

Spirulina
Nutritional Highlights: This blue-green alga boasts impressive protein levels, essential amino acids, vitamins (particularly B vitamins), iron, and other vital minerals.
Taste Profile: Distinctive marine-like flavor that can dominate if used in large quantities.
Juicing Tip: Mix with a small teaspoon of citrus or sweet fruits like pineapple to mask its strong taste.

Chlorella
Nutritional Highlights: Like spirulina, chlorella is rich in proteins, vitamins, essential fatty acids, and minerals. It's also recognized for its detoxifying properties.
Taste Profile: Green, slightly earthy, with a hint of bitterness.
Juicing Tip: Use in tandem with sweeter fruits or veggies like carrots to neutralize its bitterness.

Acai Berry
Nutritional Highlights: This berry is a powerful antioxidant, rich in essential fatty acids, dietary fiber, and vitamins.
Taste Profile: It tastes like a cross between dark chocolate and wild berries.
Juicing Tip: Given its rich berry flavor, acai pairs well with almost any fruit. For a tropical twist, combine with coconut water.

Goji Berries
Nutritional Highlights: Known as the "wolfberry", goji berries are packed with antioxidants, amino acids, vitamins, and minerals.
Taste Profile: A pleasant tangy-sweet flavor with a hint of sourness.
Juicing Tip: Soak the berries to soften and release their flavors before juicing.

Maca Root
Nutritional Highlights: Heralded for its adaptogenic properties, maca is rich in amino acids, phytonutrients, vitamins, and minerals. It's known to boost energy and stamina.
Taste Profile: Earthy and nutty with a slight malted taste.
Juicing Tip: As maca usually comes in powder form, add it after juicing and blend well. Pairs beautifully with banana and cacao for a malted flavor.

Cacao
Nutritional Highlights: Apart from the joy of chocolate, raw cacao packs a punch with antioxidants, magnesium, and other minerals. It also contains theobromine, which can boost mood.
Taste Profile: Deep, rich, and bitter chocolate flavor.
Juicing Tip: Given its bitterness, mix cacao with sweeter ingredients or creamy bases like almond milk for a smoothie-like consistency.

Camu Camu
Nutritional Highlights: This Amazonian berry is one of nature's highest sources of Vitamin C. It also possesses anti-inflammatory properties.
Taste Profile: Tart, tangy flavor similar to cherries or lemons.
Juicing Tip: Owing to its potent tartness, use sparingly and balance with sweeter fruits or natural sweeteners like honey.

GETTING STARTED

PREPARING INGREDIENTS FOR JUICING

When you've selected the right ingredients for your juicing journey, it's crucial to know how to prepare them to ensure the best taste, nutritional value, and juicer efficiency. Proper preparation makes the juicing process smoother and maximizes the benefits you gain from your juice. Here are some fundamental steps to ensure you're prepping your ingredients the right way:

Washing and Cleaning:
Always thoroughly wash your fruits and vegetables to remove dirt, pesticides, or contaminants. Use cold water and, if possible, a natural fruit and vegetable wash or a mixture of water and vinegar.
You should use a soft scrub brush to clean all the nooks and crannies of root vegetables like carrots and beets.

Peeling and Deseeding:
Some fruits and vegetables have harsh, bitter, or non-edible skins and seeds. For example, you'd typically want to peel oranges, but apples can be juiced with their skin on.
Remove seeds from fruits such as apples and pears since they can taste bitter and contain compounds not beneficial in large quantities. However, you can directly juice tiny seeds from fruits like watermelon or berries.

Cutting and Chopping:
Size matters! Large chunks can clog your juicer or reduce its efficiency. Chop ingredients into pieces that easily fit into your juicer's feed chute.
The manner of cutting can affect the juice extraction.

Temperature:
Room-temperature ingredients are generally best for juicing. Cold produce can reduce the efficiency of some juicers. If you've stored your fruits and vegetables in the fridge, it's a good idea to take them out 30 minutes to an hour before juicing.

Consider Organic:
If you're concerned about pesticides, consider buying organic produce, especially fruits and vegetables you don't peel. If buying entirely organic isn't feasible, focus on the "Dirty Dozen" – the list of produce that typically has the highest pesticide residues.

Leafy Greens:
Remove any tough stems or ribs for greens like spinach, kale, or chard, as they can be hard to process and might introduce a bitter taste.

By dedicating a little time and care to prepare your ingredients correctly, you'll extract the maximum amount of nutrients from your produce while enjoying a smoother, more flavorful juice. Always remember the quality of your juice begins with the quality and preparation of your ingredients.

PROPER STORAGE PRACTICES

It's no secret that storing freshly made juices is essential. Proper storage not only ensures that you preserve the nutritional content of your ingredients and concoctions but also prevents waste, saves money, and guarantees a fresh, delicious taste every time. Here's what you need to know:

Choosing the Right Containers:
Opt for glass containers with airtight seals for your juices. These containers are non-reactive, meaning they won't transfer harmful chemicals into your juice.
Consider using vacuum-sealed containers if you're storing juices for over a day. These reduce the amount of oxygen in contact with your juice, which can degrade its nutritional value and taste.

Storing Fresh Produce:
Keep your fruits and vegetables in the refrigerator's crisper drawer. This helps maintain humidity levels that are conducive to preserving freshness.
Some produce items, like tomatoes and bananas, are best stored at room temperature.
Remove any spoiled produce immediately, as one rotten item can quickly spoil the rest.

Juice Lifespan:
Freshly squeezed juices ideally should be consumed within the first half-hour hours. However, with proper storage and removing all the air from the container, some juices can last up to 48-72 hours.
Always store your juice in the refrigerator unless you're consuming it immediately.

Freezing for Longevity:
If you've made a large batch of juice or want to prepare in advance, consider freezing it. Fill the juice into ice cube trays or freezable containers, leaving space at the top for expansion.
When ready to consume, let the juice thaw in the fridge or at room temperature. While freezing may cause a slight degradation in texture and flavor, the nutritional content remains largely intact.

Labeling and Rotation:
Always label your juice containers with the date of preparation. This ensures that you always consume the oldest juice first and can keep track of its freshness.
Regularly rotate the produce in your refrigerator, moving older items to the front so they get used first.

Keep It Clean:
Always ensure that your storage containers are clean before storing your juice. Bacteria and mold can increase in unwashed containers, ruining juice and possibly making you ill.
It's also vital to thoroughly wash your hands and all juicing equipment before and after use.
Proper storage practices in juicing aren't just about prolonging shelf life; they're about maximizing health benefits, flavor, and the overall juicing experience.

BASIC RECIPES

DIGESTIVE HEALTH

Soothing Minty Melon Juice

Yield: 4 servings | Prep time: 10 minutes | Cook time: 2 minutes
Ingredients:
- 500g honeydew melon, peeled and cubed
- 100g fresh mint leaves

Directions:
1. Wash and prepare the honeydew melon and mint leaves.
2. Add the fresh mint leaves to the juicer.
3. Run the honeydew melon through a juicer.
4. Pour the juice into glasses and serve immediately.

Nutritional information (per 100g): 35 calories, 0.5g protein, 8.5g carbohydrates, 0.1g fat, 0.5g fiber, 0mg cholesterol, 10mg sodium, 180mg potassium.

Pear and Parsley Potion

Yield: 4 servings | Prep time: 10 minutes | Cook time: 2 minutes
Ingredients:
- 400g pears, cored
- 100g fresh parsley

Directions:
1. Prepare the pears by removing the core and slicing them.
2. Wash the parsley thoroughly.
3. Juice the pears and parsley together.
4. Pour into glasses and serve immediately.

Nutritional information (per 100g): 42 calories, 0.4g protein, 11.2g carbohydrates, 0.1g fat, 3.1g fiber, 0mg cholesterol, 7mg sodium, 119mg potassium.

Refreshing Watermelon & Basil Blend

Yield: 4 servings | Prep time: 10 minutes | Cook time: 2 minutes
Ingredients:
- 800g watermelon, rind removed, cut into chunks
- 50g fresh basil leaves

Directions:
1. Prepare watermelon chunks, ensuring rinds are removed.
2. Wash and gently pat dry fresh basil leaves.
3. Add the fresh basil leaves to the juicer.
4. Start juicing the watermelon chunks through the juicer.
5. Once juiced, stir the mixture gently and pour into glasses for immediate serving.

Nutritional information (per 100g): 30 calories, 0.6g protein, 7.6g carbohydrates, 0.2g fat, 0.4g fiber, 0mg cholesterol, 1mg sodium, 112mg potassium.

Ginger Tummy Tamer

Yield: 3 servings | Prep time: 10 minutes | Cook time: 2 minutes
Ingredients:
- 300g carrots
- 20g ginger root
- 200ml water

Directions:
1. Wash and peel the carrots and ginger.
2. Cut the carrots into manageable pieces for the juicer.
3. Feed the carrots and ginger root through the juicer.
4. Dilute with 200ml of water and stir.
5. Pour into glasses and serve.

Nutritional information (per 100g): 27 calories, 0.6g protein, 6.3g carbohydrates, 0.2g fat, 1.8g fiber, 0mg cholesterol, 58mg sodium, 195mg potassium.

Apple and Fennel Fusion

Yield: 4 servings | Prep time: 10 minutes | Cook time: 2 minutes
Ingredients:
- 400g apples, cored
- 100g fennel bulb

Directions:
1. Prepare apples by removing the core and cutting them into slices.
2. Clean and slice the fennel bulb.
3. Combine both apples and fennel in the juicer.
4. Pour the combined juice into glasses and serve.

Nutritional information (per 100g): 42 calories, 0.3g protein, 11g carbohydrates, 0.2g fat, 2.1g fiber, 0mg cholesterol, 3mg sodium, 134mg potassium.

Tropical Digestive Soother

Yield: 4 servings | Prep time: 10 minutes | Cook time: 2 minutes
Ingredients:
- 300g fresh pineapple, peeled and cored
- 200g papaya, deseeded and peeled
- 30g fresh ginger root
- 150ml coconut water

Directions:
1. Prepare the pineapple and papaya by peeling and removing the seeds.
2. Peel the ginger root.
3. Run the pineapple, papaya, and ginger through the juicer.
4. Mix in coconut water for a hydrating effect.
5. Stir well and serve chilled.

Nutritional information (per 100g): 38 calories, 0.6g protein, 9g carbohydrates, 0.2g fat, 1.4g fiber, 0mg cholesterol, 25mg sodium, 182mg potassium.

Digestive Green Bliss

Yield: 3 servings | Prep time: 10 minutes | Cook time: 2 minutes
Ingredients:
- 250g cucumber
- 250g zucchini
- 150g green apples, cored
- 20g fresh mint leaves
- 100ml water

Directions:
1. Wash the cucumber, zucchini, and green apples thoroughly.
2. Core the apples and slice them into manageable pieces.
3. Run the cucumber, zucchini, apples, and fresh mint leaves through the juicer.
4. Add water to the juice to achieve the desired consistency.
5. Stir well and serve immediately.

Nutritional information (per 100g): 24 calories, 0.8g protein, 5.6g carbohydrates, 0.2g fat, 1.2g fiber, 0mg cholesterol, 8mg sodium, 165mg potassium.

Tropical Tummy Soothe

Yield: 4 servings | Prep time: 15 minutes | Cook time: 2 minutes
Ingredients:
- 500g pineapple, peeled and cored
- 200g papaya, seeds removed

Directions:
1. Prepare the fruits by peeling and coring.
2. Feed them through the juicer.
3. Pour the juice into glasses and enjoy.

Nutritional information (per 100g): 45 calories, 0.5g protein, 11g carbohydrates, 0.2g fat, 1.2g fiber, 0mg cholesterol, 5mg sodium, 120mg potassium.

Radiant Root Refresher

Yield: 3 servings | Prep time: 10 minutes | Cook time: 2 minutes
Ingredients:
- 400g carrots
- 20g fresh turmeric root

Directions:
1. Wash and peel the carrots and turmeric.
2. Juice them together.
3. Stir and serve for a vibrant, healthful drink.

Nutritional information (per 100g): 32 calories, 0.7g protein, 8g carbohydrates, 0.2g fat, 2.4g fiber, 0mg cholesterol, 55mg sodium, 290mg potassium.

Pear-fact Digestive Elixir

Yield: 4 servings | Prep time: 10 minutes | Cook time: 2 minutes
Ingredients:
- 500g ripe pears
- 10g fresh mint leaves

Directions:
1. Wash, core, and slice the pears.
2. Feed the pears and fresh mint through the juicer.
3. Pour the juice into glasses and serve chilled.

Nutritional information (per 100g): 40 calories, 0.3g protein, 11g carbohydrates, 0.1g fat, 2.4g fiber, 0mg cholesterol, 1mg sodium, 116mg potassium.

Ginger Tummy Tonic

Yield: 2 servings | Prep time: 10 minutes | Cook time: 2 minutes.
Ingredients:
- 30g fresh ginger root
- 2 apples (approx. 300g)
- 20ml lemon juice
- 150ml water

Directions:
1. Peel and slice the ginger root.
2. Wash and chop the apples.
3. Juice the ginger and apples together.
4. Mix in the lemon juice and water.
5. Stir well and serve immediately.

Nutritional information (per 100g): 40 calories, 0.2g protein, 10g carbohydrates, 0.1g fat, 1.2g fiber, 0mg cholesterol, 3mg sodium, 80mg potassium.

Pineapple Digestive Delight

Yield: 3 servings | Prep time: 15 minutes | Cook time: 2 minutes.
Ingredients:
- 350g pineapple
- 20g fresh mint leaves
- 150ml coconut water

Directions:
1. Peel and chop the pineapple.
2. Juice the pineapple.
3. Blend the pineapple juice with mint leaves using a blender.
4. Mix with coconut water and stir.
5. Serve chilled.

Nutritional information (per 100g): 28 calories, 0.3g protein, 7g carbohydrates, 0.1g fat, 0.5g fiber, 0mg cholesterol, 15mg sodium, 90mg potassium.

Beetroot Digestive Boost

Yield: 2 servings | Prep time: 10 minutes | Cook time: 2 minutes.
Ingredients:
- 200g beetroot
- 1 cucumber (approx. 150g)
- 20ml lemon juice
- 100ml water

Directions:
1. Wash and peel the beetroot and cucumber.
2. Juice both together.
3. Add lemon juice and water.
4. Stir well and serve.

Nutritional information (per 100g): 25 calories, 1g protein, 5.5g carbohydrates, 0.2g fat, 1.5g fiber, 0mg cholesterol, 35mg sodium, 125mg potassium.

Fennel Fresh Flush

Yield: 2 servings | Prep time: 10 minutes | Cook time: 2 minutes.
Ingredients:
- 100g fennel bulb
- 2 carrots (approx. 200g)
- 1 apple (approx. 150g)
- 100ml water

Directions:
1. Wash and chop the fennel, carrots, and apple.
2. Juice all ingredients together.
3. Mix with water to reach the desired consistency.
4. Stir and serve.

Nutritional information (per 100g): 30 calories, 0.7g protein, 7g carbohydrates, 0.2g fat, 1.8g fiber, 0mg cholesterol, 20mg sodium, 130mg potassium.

Celery Digestive Calm

Yield: 3 servings | Prep time: 10 minutes | Cook time: 2 minutes.
Ingredients:
- 300g celery stalks
- 1 pear (approx. 180g)
- 20ml lime juice
- 150ml water

Directions:
1. Wash the celery stalks and pear.
2. Juice both ingredients.
3. Add lime juice and water.
4. Stir and serve immediately.

Nutritional information (per 100g): 20 calories, 0.6g protein, 5g carbohydrates, 0.2g fat, 1.4g fiber, 0mg cholesterol, 40mg sodium, 110mg potassium.

Tummy Soothing Turmeric Tonic

Yield: 2 servings | Prep time: 10 minutes | Cook time: 3 minutes.
Ingredients:
- 30g fresh turmeric root
- 1 orange (approx. 130g)
- 100ml carrot juice
- 20ml lemon juice

Directions:
1. Peel the turmeric root and orange.
2. Juice the turmeric and orange.
3. Mix in the carrot and lemon juice.
4. Stir well and serve.

Nutritional information (per 100g): 32 calories, 0.6g protein, 7.5g carbohydrates, 0.2g fat, 1.3g fiber, 0mg cholesterol, 20mg sodium, 135mg potassium.

Digestive Green Goddess

Yield: 2 servings | Prep time: 15 minutes | Cook time: 2 minutes.
Ingredients:
- 200g spinach
- 1 cucumber (approx. 150g)
- 1 kiwi (approx. 100g)
- 20ml lime juice
- 100ml water

Directions:
1. Wash all the ingredients.
2. Juice the spinach, cucumber, and kiwi.
3. Add lime juice and water.
4. Stir well and serve chilled.

Nutritional information (per 100g): 25 calories, 1.1g protein, 5.5g carbohydrates, 0.3g fat, 1.6g fiber, 0mg cholesterol, 20mg sodium, 180mg potassium.

Peppermint Digestive Pleaser

Yield: 2 servings | Prep time: 10 minutes | Cook time: 2 minutes.
Ingredients:
- 30g fresh mint leaves
- 2 green apples (approx. 300g)
- 20ml lemon juice
- 150ml water

Directions:
1. Wash the mint leaves and apples.
2. Juice both together.
3. Add lemon juice and water.
4. Stir and serve.

Nutritional information (per 100g): 35 calories, 0.3g protein, 8.5g carbohydrates, 0.2g fat, 1.4g fiber, 0mg cholesterol, 10mg sodium, 85mg potassium.

Digestive Zesty Zinger

Yield: 3 servings | Prep time: 15 minutes | Cook time: 2 minutes.
Ingredients:
200g carrots
- 1 grapefruit (approx. 300g)
- 30g fresh ginger root
- 150ml water

Directions:
1. Wash and peel the carrots and ginger.
2. Juice the carrots, grapefruit, and ginger.
3. Add water to adjust consistency.
4. Stir and serve.

Nutritional information (per 100g): 30 calories, 0.7g protein, 7g carbohydrates, 0.2g fat, 1.5g fiber, 0mg cholesterol, 25mg sodium, 140mg potassium.

Aloe & Cucumber Cooler

Yield: 2 servings | Prep time: 10 minutes | Cook time: 2 minutes.
Ingredients:
- 100ml aloe vera juice (preferably fresh)
- 1 cucumber (approx. 150g)
- 20ml lemon juice
- 100ml water

Directions:
1. Wash the cucumber.
2. Juice the cucumber.
3. Mix with aloe vera juice, lemon juice, and water.
4. Stir and serve immediately.

Nutritional information (per 100g): 15 calories, 0.4g protein, 3.5g carbohydrates, 0.1g fat, 0.6g fiber, 0mg cholesterol, 10mg sodium, 75mg potassium.

IMMUNE SYSTEM BOOST

Citrus Immune Explosion

Yield: 2 servings | Prep time: 10 minutes | Cook time: 2 minutes.
Ingredients:
- 2 oranges (approx. 260g)
- 1 grapefruit (approx. 300g)
- 20ml lemon juice
- 150ml water

Directions:
1. Peel and chop the oranges and grapefruit.
2. Juice the citrus fruits.
3. Mix in the lemon juice and water.
4. Stir well and serve immediately.

Nutritional information (per 100g): 35 calories, 0.7g protein, 8.6g carbohydrates, 0.2g fat, 1g fiber, 0mg cholesterol, 1mg sodium, 140mg potassium.

Vitamin C Surge

Yield: 3 servings | Prep time: 10 minutes | Cook time: 2 minutes.
Ingredients:
- 3 kiwis (approx. 300g)
- 1 orange (approx. 200g)
- 200ml water

Directions:
1. Peel and chop the fruits.
2. Juice them together.
3. Add water, stir, and serve.

Nutritional information (per 100g): 50 calories, 1g protein, 11g carbohydrates, 0.3g fat, 2g fiber, 0mg cholesterol, 3mg sodium, 115mg potassium.

Kale & Kiwi Kick

Yield: 2 servings | Prep time: 10 minutes | Cook time: 2 minutes.
Ingredients:
- 200g kale
- 2 kiwis (approx. 200g)
- 20ml lime juice
- 150ml water

Directions:
1. Wash the kale and kiwis.
2. Peel the kiwis.
3. Juice the kale and kiwis together.
4. Add lime juice and water.
5. Stir and serve.

Nutritional information (per 100g): 35 calories, 1.3g protein, 7g carbohydrates, 0.5g fat, 1.8g fiber, 0mg cholesterol, 25mg sodium, 190mg potassium.

Berry Immune Boost

Yield: 3 servings | Prep time: 15 minutes | Cook time: 2 minutes.
Ingredients:
- 100g strawberries
- 100g blueberries
- 100g raspberries
- 1 kiwi (approx. 100g)
- 150ml water

Directions:
1. Wash all the berries and kiwi.
2. Peel the kiwi.
3. Juice all ingredients together.
4. Add water for desired consistency.
5. Stir and serve chilled.

Nutritional information (per 100g): 30 calories, 0.6g protein, 7g carbohydrates, 0.3g fat, 2g fiber, 0mg cholesterol, 2mg sodium, 115mg potassium.

Pineapple Ginger Punch

Yield: 3 servings | Prep time: 15 minutes | Cook time: 2 minutes.
Ingredients:
- 350g pineapple
- 30g fresh ginger root
- 150ml coconut water

Directions:
1. Peel and chop the pineapple.
2. Juice the pineapple and ginger together.
3. Mix with coconut water.
4. Stir and serve chilled.

Nutritional information (per 100g): 35 calories, 0.4g protein, 8.5g carbohydrates, 0.2g fat, 0.5g fiber, 0mg cholesterol, 15mg sodium, 90mg potassium.

Green Immunity Guardian

Yield: 2 servings | Prep time: 10 minutes | Cook time: 2 minutes.
Ingredients:
- 200g spinach
- 1 green apple (approx. 150g)
- 20ml lemon juice
- 20g fresh ginger root
- 100ml water

Directions:
1. Wash the spinach, apple, and ginger.
2. Juice the spinach, apple, and ginger together.
3. Add lemon juice and water.
4. Stir well and serve.

Nutritional information (per 100g): 25 calories, 1g protein, 6g carbohydrates, 0.2g fat, 1.6g fiber, 0mg cholesterol, 20mg sodium, 125mg potassium.

Turmeric Immune Elixir

Yield: 2 servings | Prep time: 10 minutes | Cook time: 2 minutes.
Ingredients:

- 30g fresh turmeric root
- 1 orange (approx. 130g)
- 20ml lemon juice
- 1 carrot (approx. 100g)
- 100ml water

Directions:

1. Peel the turmeric, orange, and carrot.
2. Juice the ingredients together.
3. Add lemon juice and water.
4. Stir well and serve immediately.

Nutritional information (per 100g): 30 calories, 0.7g protein, 7.2g carbohydrates, 0.2g fat, 1.4g fiber, 0mg cholesterol, 25mg sodium, 140mg potassium.

Papaya Immunity Paradise

Yield: 2 servings | Prep time: 10 minutes | Cook time: 2 minutes.
Ingredients:

- 250g papaya
- 1 orange (approx. 130g)
- 20ml lemon juice
- 100ml water

Directions:

1. Peel and deseed the papaya.
2. Juice the papaya and orange.
3. Add lemon juice and water.
4. Stir and serve.

Nutritional information (per 100g): 35 calories, 0.6g protein, 8g carbohydrates, 0.3g fat, 1.2g fiber, 0mg cholesterol, 10mg sodium, 110mg potassium.

Red Radish Refresher

Yield: 2 servings | Prep time: 10 minutes | Cook time: 2 minutes.
Ingredients:

- 100g red radishes
- 2 apples (approx. 300g)
- 20ml lemon juice
- 150ml water

Directions:

1. Wash the radishes and apples.
2. Juice both ingredients.
3. Add lemon juice and water.
4. Stir and serve.

Nutritional information (per 100g): 40 calories, 0.3g protein, 10g carbohydrates, 0.2g fat, 1.4g fiber, 0mg cholesterol, 15mg sodium, 80mg potassium.

Immune Boosting Beet Blend

Yield: 2 servings | Prep time: 15 minutes | Cook time: 2 minutes.
Ingredients:
- 200g beetroot
- 1 carrot (approx. 100g)
- 20g fresh ginger root
- 150ml water

Directions:
1. Wash and peel the beetroot, carrot, and ginger.
2. Juice all ingredients.
3. Add water for desired consistency.
4. Stir and serve.

Nutritional information (per 100g): 30 calories, 1g protein, 7g carbohydrates, 0.2g fat, 1.6g fiber, 0mg cholesterol, 30mg sodium, 140mg potassium.

Cucumber & Mint Immunity Mix

Yield: 3 servings | Prep time: 10 minutes | Cook time: 2 minutes.
Ingredients:
- 200g cucumber
- 30g fresh mint leaves
- 1 apple (approx. 150g)
- 150ml water

Directions:
1. Wash the cucumber, mint, and apple.
2. Juice all ingredients.
3. Add water to achieve the desired consistency.
4. Stir and serve chilled.

Nutritional information (per 100g): 25 calories, 0.5g protein, 6g carbohydrates, 0.2g fat, 1.2g fiber, 0mg cholesterol, 10mg sodium, 85mg potassium.

Berry Blast

Yield: 4 servings | Prep time: 10 minutes | Cook time: 2 minutes.
Ingredients:
- 200g blueberries
- 200g strawberries
- 150g raspberries
- 1 beetroot (approx. 150g)
- 500ml water

Directions:
1. Wash and prep all the fruits.
2. Combine fruits in the juicer.
3. Add water and blend.
4. Serve and enjoy.

Nutritional information (per 100g): 50 calories, 1g protein, 12g carbohydrates, 0.3g fat, 2g fiber, 0mg cholesterol, 5mg sodium, 80mg potassium.

Tropical Immunity Wave

Yield: 4 servings | Prep time: 15 minutes | Cook time: 2 minutes.
Ingredients:
- 200g pineapple
- 2 kiwis (approx. 200g)
- 200g papaya
- 50g spinach
- 500ml coconut water

Directions:
1. Prep and chop the fruits.
2. Place fruits and spinach in the juicer.
3. Add coconut water and blend until smooth.
4. Serve chilled.

Nutritional information (per 100g): 40 calories, 0.6g protein, 9g carbohydrates, 0.2g fat, 1g fiber, 0mg cholesterol, 30mg sodium, 110mg potassium.

Citrus Immune Booster

Yield: 3 servings | Prep time: 10 minutes | Cook time: 2 minutes.
Ingredients:
- 2 oranges (approx. 400g)
- 1 grapefruit (approx. 300g)
- 1 lemon (approx. 100g)
- 30g turmeric root
- 300ml water

Directions:
1. Peel the citrus fruits and chop them.
2. Grate the turmeric root.
3. Combine all ingredients in a juicer.
4. Blend until smooth.
5. Serve chilled.

Nutritional information (per 100g): 45 calories, 0.7g protein, 11g carbohydrates, 0.1g fat, 1g fiber, 0mg cholesterol, 2mg sodium, 140mg potassium.

Energy boost

Yield: 4 servings | Prep time: 15 minutes | Cook time: 2 minutes.
Ingredients:
- 300g mixed berries (strawberries, blueberries, raspberries)
- 1 pomegranate (approx. 200g seeds)
- 500ml water

Directions:
1. Prep the fruits.
2. Extract seeds from the pomegranate.
3. Blend all ingredients in the juicer.
4. Serve and enjoy.

Nutritional information (per 100g): 45 calories, 0.7g protein, 11g carbohydrates, 0.3g fat, 1.5g fiber, 0mg cholesterol, 3mg sodium, 85mg potassium.

Rooted Immunity

Yield: 2 servings | Prep time: 10 minutes | Cook time: 2 minutes.
Ingredients:
- 2 carrots (approx. 200g)
- 1 beetroot (approx. 150g)
- 20g ginger
- 300ml water

Directions:
1. Wash, peel, and chop the ingredients.
2. Combine in the juicer.
3. Blend, pour into glasses, and serve.

Nutritional information (per 100g): 35 calories, 0.8g protein, 8g carbohydrates, 0.2g fat, 2g fiber, 0mg cholesterol, 40mg sodium, 95mg potassium.

Gingered Green Goodness

Yield: 3 servings | Prep time: 10 minutes | Cook time: 2 minutes.
Ingredients:
- 200g spinach
- 1 cucumber (approx. 300g)
- 1 green apple (approx. 200g)
- 30g ginger
- 300ml water

Directions:
1. Wash and chop all ingredients.
2. Place them in the juicer.
3. Blend until smooth and serve immediately.

Nutritional information (per 100g): 25 calories, 0.7g protein, 5g carbohydrates, 0.2g fat, 0.8g fiber, 0mg cholesterol, 15mg sodium, 90mg potassium.

Green Defender Delight

Yield: 4 servings | Prep time: 15 minutes | Cook time: 2 minutes.
Ingredients:
- 200g kale
- 2 green apples (approx. 400g)
- 3 sticks celery (approx. 150g)
- 2cm piece of ginger
- 500ml water

Directions:
1. Wash and chop the kale, apples, celery, and ginger.
2. Place the ingredients into a juicer.
3. Add water and blend until smooth.
4. Pour the juice through a strainer to remove any pulp.
5. Serve immediately and enjoy.

Nutritional information (per 100g): 40 calories, 0.5g protein, 9g carbohydrates, 0.2g fat, 1.2g fiber, 0mg cholesterol, 10mg sodium, 115mg potassium.

Melon Mint Marvel

Yield: 4 servings | Prep time: 10 minutes | Cook time: 2 minutes.
Ingredients:
- 1 small watermelon (approx. 800g without rind)
- 50g fresh mint leaves
- 400ml water

Directions:
1. Chop the watermelon into chunks.
2. Combine watermelon, mint, and water in the juicer.
3. Blend until smooth and serve chilled.

Nutritional information (per 100g): 30 calories, 0.6g protein, 7g carbohydrates, 0.2g fat, 0.4g fiber, 0mg cholesterol, 2mg sodium, 90mg potassium.

Pineapple Paradise

Yield: 3 servings | Prep time: 10 minutes | Cook time: 2 minutes.
Ingredients:
- 500g pineapple
- 1 lemon (approx. 100g)
- 300ml water

Directions:
1. Chop the pineapple.
2. Juice the lemon.
3. Combine all ingredients in the juicer, blend, and serve.

Nutritional information (per 100g): 40 calories, 0.5g protein, 10g carbohydrates, 0.2g fat, 0.5g fiber, 0mg cholesterol, 2mg sodium, 85mg potassium.

DETOXIFICATION

Romaine & Raspberry Rejuvenator

Yield: 2 servings | Prep time: 10 minutes | Cook time: 2 minutes.
Ingredients:
- 200g romaine lettuce
- 100g raspberries
- 20ml lemon juice
- 150ml water

Directions:
1. Wash the romaine lettuce and raspberries.
2. Juice them together.
3. Add lemon juice and water.
4. Stir and serve chilled.

Nutritional information (per 100g): 15 calories, 1g protein, 3.5g carbohydrates, 0.2g fat, 1.8g fiber, 0mg cholesterol, 10mg sodium, 90mg potassium.

Pineapple Charcoal Purify

Yield: 2 servings | Prep time: 15 minutes | Cook time: 3 minutes.
Ingredients:
- 250g pineapple
- 1 tsp activated charcoal powder
- 150ml coconut water

Directions:
1. Peel and chop the pineapple.
2. Juice the pineapple.
3. Mix pineapple juice, charcoal powder, and coconut water.
4. Stir well until charcoal is dissolved, and serve.

Nutritional information (per 100g): 30 calories, 0.3g protein, 7g carbohydrates, 0.2g fat, 0.5g fiber, 0mg cholesterol, 20mg sodium, 105mg potassium.

Celery Detox Delight

Yield: 3 servings | Prep time: 10 minutes | Cook time: 2 minutes.
Ingredients:
- 400g celery stalks
- 20ml lemon juice
- 150ml water

Directions:
1. Wash the celery stalks.
2. Juice the celery.
3. Add lemon juice and water.
4. Stir well and serve immediately.

Nutritional information (per 100g): 10 calories, 0.5g protein, 2.5g carbohydrates, 0.1g fat, 1g fiber, 0mg cholesterol, 50mg sodium, 80mg potassium.

Turmeric Flush Elixir

Yield: 2 servings | Prep time: 10 minutes | Cook time: 2 minutes.
Ingredients:
- 30g fresh turmeric root
- 1 orange (approx. 130g)
- 150ml carrot juice
- 20ml lemon juice

Directions:
1. Peel the turmeric and orange.
2. Juice the turmeric and orange.
3. Mix with carrot and lemon juice.
4. Stir well and serve.

Nutritional information (per 100g): 28 calories, 0.6g protein, 6.5g carbohydrates, 0.2g fat, 1.3g fiber, 0mg cholesterol, 25mg sodium, 135mg potassium.

Tangy Tomato Cleanse

Yield: 2 servings | Prep time: 10 minutes | Cook time: 2 minutes.
Ingredients:
- 400g tomatoes
- 1 celery stalk (approx. 50g)
- 20ml lemon juice
- A pinch of Himalayan pink salt

Directions:
1. Wash the tomatoes and celery stalk.
2. Juice both ingredients.
3. Add lemon juice and a pinch of salt.
4. Stir and serve chilled.

Nutritional information (per 100g): 15 calories, 0.6g protein, 3.5g carbohydrates, 0.2g fat, 1g fiber, 0mg cholesterol, 20mg sodium, 150mg potassium.

Spicy Green Detox

Yield: 2 servings | Prep time: 10 minutes | Cook time: 2 minutes.
Ingredients:
- 200g spinach
- 1 green apple (approx. 150g)
- 1 small green chili (approx. 10g)
- 150ml water

Directions:
1. Wash the spinach, apple, and green chili.
2. Juice all ingredients together. (Remove the seeds from the chili for less heat).
3. Add water to achieve the desired consistency.
4. Stir and serve immediately.

Nutritional information (per 100g): 20 calories, 1g protein, 4.5g carbohydrates, 0.2g fat, 1.5g fiber, 0mg cholesterol, 20mg sodium, 115mg potassium.

Cooling Cilantro Detox

Yield: 2 servings | Prep time: 10 minutes | Cook time: 2 minutes.
Ingredients:
- 30g fresh cilantro (coriander)
- 2 cucumbers (approx. 300g)
- 20ml lime juice
- 150ml water

Directions:
1. Wash the cilantro and cucumbers.
2. Juice both ingredients.
3. Add lime juice and water.
4. Stir and serve chilled.

Nutritional information (per 100g): 10 calories, 0.6g protein, 2.5g carbohydrates, 0.1g fat, 0.8g fiber, 0mg cholesterol, 5mg sodium, 95mg potassium.

Sweet Beet Detoxifier

Yield: 2 servings | Prep time: 10 minutes | Cook time: 2 minutes.
Ingredients:
- 200g beetroot
- 2 pears (approx. 360g)
- 150ml water

Directions:
1. Wash and peel the beetroot.
2. Wash and core the pears.
3. Juice both ingredients.
4. Add water for desired consistency.
5. Stir and serve.

Nutritional information (per 100g): 35 calories, 0.6g protein, 8g carbohydrates, 0.2g fat, 2g fiber, 0mg cholesterol, 25mg sodium, 130mg potassium.

Carrot & Fennel Fusion

Yield: 2 servings | Prep time: 10 minutes | Cook time: 2 minutes.
Ingredients:
- 200g carrots
- 100g fennel bulb
- 20ml orange juice
- 100ml water

Directions:
1. Wash and peel the carrots.
2. Wash and chop the fennel bulb.
3. Juice the carrots and fennel together.
4. Mix with orange juice and water.
5. Stir and serve immediately.

Nutritional information (per 100g): 28 calories, 0.7g protein, 6.5g carbohydrates, 0.3g fat, 2g fiber, 0mg cholesterol, 40mg sodium, 210mg potassium.

Luscious Lime & Basil Booster

Yield: 2 servings | Prep time: 10 minutes | Cook time: 2 minutes.
Ingredients:
- 40ml lime juice
- 20g fresh basil leaves
- 1 pear (approx. 180g)
- 150ml water

Directions:
1. Wash the basil leaves.
2. Wash and core the pear.
3. Juice the basil and pear.
4. Mix with lime juice and water.
5. Stir and serve chilled.

Nutritional information (per 100g): 25 calories, 0.4g protein, 6g carbohydrates, 0.1g fat, 1.4g fiber, 0mg cholesterol, 10mg sodium, 80mg potassium.

Detox Dreamer

Yield: 4 servings | Prep time: 10 minutes | Cook time: 3 minutes.
Ingredients:
- 300g kale
- 1 cucumber (approx. 250g)
- 2 green apples (approx. 400g)
- 20g parsley
- 500ml water

Directions:
1. Wash and chop all the ingredients.
2. Combine them in a juicer.
3. Blend until smooth.
4. Serve immediately.

Nutritional information (per 100g): 35 calories, 1.1g protein, 8g carbohydrates, 0.3g fat, 1.5g fiber, 0mg cholesterol, 12mg sodium, 120mg potassium.

Beet Bliss

Yield: 3 servings | Prep time: 10 minutes | Cook time: 2 minutes.
Ingredients:
- 3 beetroots (approx. 450g)
- 2 carrots (approx. 200g)
- 300ml water

Directions:
1. Peel and chop the beetroots and carrots.
2. Juice the ingredients together.
3. Add water, stir, and serve.

Nutritional information (per 100g): 40 calories, 1g protein, 9g carbohydrates, 0.2g fat, 2g fiber, 0mg cholesterol, 35mg sodium, 130mg potassium.

Lemon Ginger Glow

Yield: 2 servings | Prep time: 5 minutes | Cook time: 2 minutes.
Ingredients:
- 2 lemons (approx. 200g)
- 30g ginger root
- 300ml water

Directions:
1. Juice the lemons.
2. Grate the ginger root.
3. Mix lemon juice, ginger, and water in a pitcher.
4. Serve chilled.

Nutritional information (per 100g): 20 calories, 0.5g protein, 6g carbohydrates, 0.2g fat, 0.8g fiber, 0mg cholesterol, 2mg sodium, 60mg potassium.

Cranberry Cleanse

Yield: 4 servings | Prep time: 10 minutes | Cook time: 2 minutes.
Ingredients:
- 500g cranberries
- 1 orange (approx. 200g)
- 500ml water

Directions:
1. Juice the cranberries and orange together.
2. Combine with water in a pitcher.
3. Chill and serve.

Nutritional information (per 100g): 30 calories, 0.4g protein, 7g carbohydrates, 0.1g fat, 1.2g fiber, 0mg cholesterol, 3mg sodium, 55mg potassium.

Chard Charge

Yield: 4 servings | Prep time: 15 minutes | Cook time: 2 minutes.
Ingredients:
- 300g swiss chard
- 2 pears (approx. 400g)
- 1 lemon (approx. 100g)
- 500ml water

Directions:
1. Wash and chop the chard and pears.
2. Juice all ingredients.
3. Add water, blend, and serve.

Nutritional information (per 100g): 35 calories, 0.7g protein, 9g carbohydrates, 0.2g fat, 1.3g fiber, 0mg cholesterol, 10mg sodium, 90mg potassium.

Celery Clean Slate

Yield: 3 servings | Prep time: 10 minutes | Cook time: 2 minutes.
Ingredients:
- 5 celery stalks (approx. 300g)
- 1 cucumber (approx. 250g)
- 300ml water

Directions:
1. Wash and chop celery and cucumber.
2. Juice them together.
3. Mix with water and serve.

Nutritional information (per 100g): 15 calories, 0.6g protein, 3g carbohydrates, 0.1g fat, 0.8g fiber, 0mg cholesterol, 20mg sodium, 70mg potassium.

Pomegranate Power Punch

Yield: 4 servings | Prep time: 15 minutes | Cook time: 2 minutes.
Ingredients:
- 4 pomegranates (approx. 800g seeds)
- 1 lime (approx. 50g)
- 500ml water

Directions:
1. Extract seeds from the pomegranates.
2. Juice pomegranate seeds and lime.
3. Add water, stir, and serve.

Nutritional information (per 100g): 50 calories, 0.8g protein, 11g carbohydrates, 0.3g fat, 1.2g fiber, 0mg cholesterol, 3mg sodium, 75mg potassium.

Fennel Freshener

Yield: 3 servings | Prep time: 10 minutes | Cook time: 2 minutes.
Ingredients:
- 2 fennel bulbs (approx. 400g)
- 2 apples (approx. 400g)
- 300ml water

Directions:
1. Wash and chop the fennel and apples.
2. Juice the ingredients.
3. Add water, blend, and serve.

Nutritional information (per 100g): 40 calories, 0.7g protein, 10g carbohydrates, 0.2g fat, 1.4g fiber, 0mg cholesterol, 8mg sodium, 85mg potassium.

Broccoli Boost

Yield: 4 servings | Prep time: 15 minutes | Cook time: 2 minutes.
Ingredients:
- 300g broccoli florets
- 2 green apples (approx. 400g)
- 500ml water

Directions:
1. Wash and chop broccoli and apples.
2. Juice the ingredients.
3. Add water, blend, and serve.

Nutritional information (per 100g): 30 calories, 1g protein, 7g carbohydrates, 0.2g fat, 1.5g fiber, 0mg cholesterol, 15mg sodium, 100mg potassium.

Spinach Soothe

Yield: 3 servings | Prep time: 10 minutes | Cook time: 2 minutes.
Ingredients:
- 300g spinach
- 2 pears (approx. 400g)
- 300ml water

Directions:
1. Wash and prep the spinach and pears.
2. Juice together.
3. Mix with water and serve.

Nutritional information (per 100g): 30 calories, 0.9g protein, 7g carbohydrates, 0.2g fat, 1.3g fiber, 0mg cholesterol, 10mg sodium, 80mg potassium.

ENERGY AND VITALITY

Energizing Orange Oasis

Yield: 2 servings | Prep time: 10 minutes | Cook time: 2 minutes.
Ingredients:
- 3 oranges (approx. 390g)
- 1 carrot (approx. 100g)
- 20ml honey

Directions:
1. Peel and chop the oranges and carrot.
2. Juice both ingredients.
3. Add honey and stir until dissolved.
4. Serve immediately for a fresh burst of energy.

Nutritional information (per 100g): 40 calories, 0.9g protein, 9.6g carbohydrates, 0.2g fat, 1.3g fiber, 0mg cholesterol, 2mg sodium, 160mg potassium.

Vibrant Vitality Blend

Yield: 2 servings | Prep time: 15 minutes | Cook time: 2 minutes.
Ingredients:
- 200g strawberries
- 100g blueberries
- 1 banana (approx. 120g)
- 150ml almond milk

Directions:
1. Wash the strawberries and blueberries.
2. Peel the banana.
3. Juice the berries and blend with the banana.
4. Mix with almond milk and serve immediately.

Nutritional information (per 100g): 45 calories, 1.1g protein, 10.2g carbohydrates, 0.5g fat, 2g fiber, 0mg cholesterol, 5mg sodium, 115mg potassium.

Revitalizing Red Rush

Yield: 2 servings | Prep time: 10 minutes | Cook time: 2 minutes.
Ingredients:
- 250g watermelon
- 1 pomegranate (approx. 200g)
- 20ml lime juice

Directions:
1. Chop the watermelon into chunks and remove the seeds.
2. Extract seeds from the pomegranate.
3. Juice watermelon and pomegranate seeds together.
4. Mix with lime juice and serve immediately.

Nutritional information (per 100g): 35 calories, 0.7g protein, 8.5g carbohydrates, 0.3g fat, 1g fiber, 0mg cholesterol, 2mg sodium, 120mg potassium.

Zingy Ginger Kick

Yield: 2 servings | Prep time: 10 minutes | Cook time: 2 minutes.
Ingredients:
- 3 carrots (approx. 300g)
- 40g fresh ginger root
- 20ml lemon juice
- 150ml water

Directions:
1. Wash and peel the carrots and ginger root.
2. Juice both ingredients.
3. Mix with lemon juice and water.
4. Stir and serve for an energizing boost.

Nutritional information (per 100g): 30 calories, 0.9g protein, 7g carbohydrates, 0.2g fat, 1.8g fiber, 0mg cholesterol, 40mg sodium, 210mg potassium.

Berry Vitality Booster

Yield: 2 servings | Prep time: 10 minutes | Cook time: 2 minutes.
Ingredients:
- 150g raspberries
- 150g blackberries
- 150ml water

Directions:
1. Wash the raspberries and blackberries.
2. Juice both berries.
3. Add water to achieve the desired consistency.
4. Stir and serve chilled.

Nutritional information (per 100g): 35 calories, 1.2g protein, 8g carbohydrates, 0.5g fat, 4g fiber, 0mg cholesterol, 1mg sodium, 160mg potassium.

Moringa Magic Mix

Yield: 2 servings | Prep time: 10 minutes | Cook time: 2 minutes.
Ingredients:
- 1 apple (approx. 150g)
- 10g moringa leaves
- 20ml honey
- 150ml water

Directions:
1. Wash the apple and moringa leaves.
2. Juice both ingredients.
3. Mix with honey and water.
4. Stir until honey is dissolved and serve.

Nutritional information (per 100g): 40 calories, 0.5g protein, 10g carbohydrates, 0.3g fat, 1.2g fiber, 0mg cholesterol, 5mg sodium, 85mg potassium.

Golden Vitality Elixir

Yield: 2 servings | Prep time: 15 minutes | Cook time: 2 minutes.
Ingredients:
- 30g fresh turmeric root
- 2 oranges (approx. 260g)
- 20ml honey
- 150ml water

Directions:
1. Peel and chop the turmeric root and oranges.
2. Juice both ingredients.
3. Mix with honey and water.
4. Stir until honey is dissolved and serve.

Nutritional information (per 100g): 45 calories, 0.8g protein, 10.5g carbohydrates, 0.4g fat, 1.4g fiber, 0mg cholesterol, 3mg sodium, 165mg potassium.

Basil & Berry Vitality Blend

Yield: 2 servings | Prep time: 10 minutes | Cook time: 2 minutes.
Ingredients:
- 200g strawberries
- 30g fresh basil leaves
- 1 kiwi (approx. 100g)
- 150ml water

Directions:
1. Wash the strawberries and basil leaves.
2. Peel the kiwi.
3. Juice strawberries, basil, and kiwi.
4. Add water for desired consistency.
5. Stir and serve chilled.

Nutritional information (per 100g): 35 calories, 1g protein, 8g carbohydrates, 0.4g fat, 2g fiber, 0mg cholesterol, 5mg sodium, 140mg potassium.

Goji Berry Boost

Yield: 2 servings | Prep time: 10 minutes | Cook time: 2 minutes.
Ingredients:
- 50g goji berries
- 1 orange (approx. 130g)
- 1 carrot (approx. 100g)
- 150ml water

Directions:
1. Soak goji berries in water for 10 minutes to rehydrate.
2. Peel and chop the orange and carrot.
3. Juice the orange and carrot.
4. Blend the juice with goji berries and water.
5. Serve chilled.

Nutritional information (per 100g): 45 calories, 1.2g protein, 10g carbohydrates, 0.4g fat, 2.5g fiber, 0mg cholesterol, 15mg sodium, 200mg potassium.

Broccoli & Berry Boost

Yield: 2 servings | Prep time: 15 minutes | Cook time: 2 minutes.
Ingredients:
- 150g broccoli
- 150g mixed berries (strawberries, blueberries, raspberries)
- 20ml honey
- 150ml water

Directions:
1. Wash the broccoli and berries.
2. Juice the broccoli and berries together.
3. Add honey and water, then stir.
4. Serve chilled.

Nutritional information (per 100g): 35 calories, 1g protein, 8g carbohydrates, 0.3g fat, 2.5g fiber, 0mg cholesterol, 10mg sodium, 180mg potassium.

Vibrant Vitality Verve

Yield: 4 servings | Prep time: 15 minutes | Cook time: 2 minutes.
Ingredients:
- 300g spinach
- 2 bananas (approx. 300g)
- 2 oranges (approx. 400g)
- 500ml almond milk

Directions:
1. Wash and prep the spinach.
2. Peel the bananas and oranges.
3. Combine all ingredients in a juicer.
4. Blend until smooth and serve.

Nutritional information (per 100g): 60 calories, 1.5g protein, 13g carbohydrates, 0.7g fat, 1.8g fiber, 0mg cholesterol, 25mg sodium, 310mg potassium.

Radiant Rise

Yield: 3 servings | Prep time: 10 minutes | Cook time: 2 minutes.
Ingredients:
- 200g blueberries
- 3 kiwis (approx. 300g)
- 1 apple (approx. 200g)
- 300ml water

Directions:
1. Wash and prep the fruits.
2. Juice them together.
3. Add water, stir, and serve.

Nutritional information (per 100g): 45 calories, 0.9g protein, 10g carbohydrates, 0.3g fat, 2g fiber, 0mg cholesterol, 5mg sodium, 160mg potassium.

Powerhouse Punch

Yield: 4 servings | Prep time: 15 minutes | Cook time: 2 minutes.
Ingredients:
- 300g kale
- 1 beetroot (approx. 150g)
- 1 carrot (approx. 100g)
- 4 celery stalks (approx. 200g)
- 500ml water

Directions:
1. Wash and chop all ingredients.
2. Place them in the juicer.
3. Blend until smooth.
4. Pour into glasses and serve.

Nutritional information (per 100g): 30 calories, 1.3g protein, 7g carbohydrates, 0.2g fat, 2g fiber, 0mg cholesterol, 35mg sodium, 220mg potassium.

Energizing Elixir

Yield: 2 servings | Prep time: 10 minutes | Cook time: 2 minutes.
Ingredients:
- 200g strawberries
- 1 apple (approx. 200g)
- 1 orange (approx. 200g)
- 200ml coconut water

Directions:
1. Wash and prep the fruits.
2. Juice them together.
3. Mix with coconut water and serve.

Nutritional information (per 100g): 45 calories, 0.7g protein, 11g carbohydrates, 0.2g fat, 1.8g fiber, 0mg cholesterol, 10mg sodium, 180mg potassium.

Morning Motivator

Yield: 3 servings | Prep time: 10 minutes | Cook time: 2 minutes.
Ingredients:
- 2 oranges (approx. 400g)
- 2 bananas (approx. 300g)
- 1 tablespoon of chia seeds (approx. 15g)
- 300ml almond milk

Directions:
1. Peel the oranges and bananas.
2. Combine all ingredients in a juicer.
3. Blend until smooth and serve.

Nutritional information (per 100g): 65 calories, 1.3g protein, 15g carbohydrates, 1g fat, 2g fiber, 0mg cholesterol, 20mg sodium, 210mg potassium.

Tropical Twist

Yield: 4 servings | Prep time: 15 minutes | Cook time: 2 minutes.
Ingredients:

- 400g pineapple
- 2 mangoes (approx. 400g)
- 200ml coconut milk
- 300ml water

Directions:

1. Peel and chop the pineapple and mangoes.
2. Juice them together.
3. Add coconut milk and water. Blend and serve.

Nutritional information (per 100g): 55 calories, 0.8g protein, 12g carbohydrates, 1.2g fat, 1.5g fiber, 0mg cholesterol, 10mg sodium, 140mg potassium.

Minty Morning

Yield: 3 servings | Prep time: 10 minutes | Cook time: 2 minutes.
Ingredients:

- 1 cucumber (approx. 250g)
- 50g fresh mint leaves
- 2 limes (approx. 100g)
- 300ml water

Directions:

1. Wash and chop cucumber and mint.
2. Juice cucumber, mint, and limes together.
3. Add water, stir, and serve.

Nutritional information (per 100g): 20 calories, 0.6g protein, 5g carbohydrates, 0.1g fat, 0.9g fiber, 0mg cholesterol, 5mg sodium, 90mg potassium.

Ginger Go-Getter

Yield: 2 servings | Prep time: 10 minutes | Cook time: 2 minutes.
Ingredients:

- 2 carrots (approx. 200g)
- 2 apples (approx. 400g)
- 30g ginger root
- 200ml water

Directions:

1. Wash and chop the carrots and apples.
2. Grate the ginger root.
3. Juice all ingredients together. Blend and serve.

Nutritional information (per 100g): 40 calories, 0.5g protein, 10g carbohydrates, 0.2g fat, 1.5g fiber, 0mg cholesterol, 10mg sodium, 110mg potassium.

Breezy Berries

Yield: 4 servings | Prep time: 15 minutes | Cook time: 2 minutes.
Ingredients:
- 200g raspberries
- 200g blackberries
- 1 apple (approx. 200g)
- 500ml water

Directions:
1. Wash and prep the fruits.
2. Juice them.
3. Add water, blend, and serve.

Nutritional information (per 100g): 30 calories, 0.8g protein, 7g carbohydrates, 0.3g fat, 2g fiber, 0mg cholesterol, 5mg sodium, 120mg potassium.

Golden Green Glory

Yield: 4 servings | Prep time: 15 minutes | Cook time: 2 minutes.
Ingredients:
- 300g kale
- 1 apple (approx. 200g)
- 30g turmeric root
- 500ml green tea (brewed and cooled)

Directions:
1. Wash and chop kale and apple.
2. Grate the turmeric root.
3. Juice kale, apple, and turmeric.
4. Mix with green tea and serve.

Nutritional information (per 100g): 35 calories, 1.2g protein, 8g carbohydrates, 0.4g fat, 1.7g fiber, 0mg cholesterol, 10mg sodium, 150mg potassium.

INFLAMMATION REDUCTION

Turmeric Tonic Tranquility

Yield: 2 servings | Prep time: 10 minutes | Cook time: 2 minutes.
Ingredients:
- 40g fresh turmeric root
- 2 oranges (approx. 260g)
- 20ml lemon juice
- 150ml water

Directions:
1. Peel and chop the turmeric root and oranges.
2. Juice all ingredients together.
3. Add water and mix well.
4. Serve chilled.

Nutritional information (per 100g): 30 calories, 0.7g protein, 7g carbohydrates, 0.2g fat, 1.2g fiber, 0mg cholesterol, 2mg sodium, 125mg potassium.

Pineapple & Ginger Glow

Yield: 2 servings | Prep time: 10 minutes | Cook time: 2 minutes.
Ingredients:
- 300g pineapple
- 20g fresh ginger root
- 150ml coconut water

Directions:
1. Peel and chop the pineapple and ginger.
2. Juice both ingredients.
3. Add coconut water and stir.
4. Serve immediately.

Nutritional information (per 100g): 35 calories, 0.6g protein, 8.5g carbohydrates, 0.2g fat, 1g fiber, 0mg cholesterol, 25mg sodium, 120mg potassium.

Basil & Blueberry Bliss

Yield: 2 servings | Prep time: 10 minutes | Cook time: 2 minutes.
Ingredients:
- 150g blueberries
- 30g fresh basil leaves
- 20ml honey
- 150ml water

Directions:
1. Wash the blueberries and basil leaves.
2. Juice the blueberries and basil.
3. Add honey and water, then stir.
4. Serve immediately.

Nutritional information (per 100g): 40 calories, 0.5g protein, 10g carbohydrates, 0.3g fat, 1.5g fiber, 0mg cholesterol, 5mg sodium, 60mg potassium.

Cherry Chia Charm

Yield: 2 servings | Prep time: 15 minutes | Cook time: 2 minutes.
Ingredients:
- 250g cherries (pitted)
- 1 tsp chia seeds
- 20ml lemon juice
- 150ml almond milk

Directions:
1. Pit the cherries.
2. Blend cherries, chia seeds, lemon juice, and almond milk until smooth.
3. Allow to sit for 10 minutes for chia seeds to expand.
4. Stir and serve.

Nutritional information (per 100g): 40 calories, 1.2g protein, 8g carbohydrates, 1g fat, 2.5g fiber, 0mg cholesterol, 10mg sodium, 85mg potassium.

Flaxseed & Fig Fusion

Yield: 2 servings | Prep time: 10 minutes | Cook time: 2 minutes.
Ingredients:
- 150g figs
- 1 tsp flaxseed oil
- 20ml honey
- 150ml water

Directions:
1. Wash and chop the figs.
2. Blend figs, flaxseed oil, honey, and water until smooth.
3. Serve chilled.

Nutritional information (per 100g): 50 calories, 0.6g protein, 11g carbohydrates, 1.5g fat, 1.8g fiber, 0mg cholesterol, 2mg sodium, 85mg potassium.

Rosehip & Raspberry Relief

Yield: 2 servings | Prep time: 10 minutes | Cook time: 2 minutes.
Ingredients:
- 150g raspberries
- 20g rosehips
- 150ml water

Directions:
1. Wash the raspberries and rosehips.
2. Juice both ingredients.
3. Add water and mix well.
4. Serve chilled.

Nutritional information (per 100g): 25 calories, 1g protein, 5.5g carbohydrates, 0.2g fat, 3g fiber, 0mg cholesterol, 3mg sodium, 90mg potassium.

Beetroot & Blackberry Burst

Yield: 2 servings | Prep time: 15 minutes | Cook time: 2 minutes.
Ingredients:

- 1 beetroot (approx. 150g)
- 150g blackberries
- 150ml water

Directions:

1. Wash and chop the beetroot.
2. Wash the blackberries.
3. Juice both ingredients.
4. Add water and mix well.
5. Serve immediately.

Nutritional information (per 100g): 30 calories, 1.2g protein, 7g carbohydrates, 0.3g fat, 2.5g fiber, 0mg cholesterol, 20mg sodium, 180mg potassium.

Golden Grapefruit Glow

Yield: 2 servings | Prep time: 10 minutes | Cook time: 2 minutes.
Ingredients:

- 2 grapefruits (approx. 400g)
- 30g fresh turmeric root
- 20ml honey
- 150ml water

Directions:

1. Peel and chop the grapefruits and turmeric root.
2. Juice both ingredients.
3. Mix in honey and water.
4. Stir well and serve chilled.

Nutritional information (per 100g): 35 calories, 0.7g protein, 8.5g carbohydrates, 0.2g fat, 1.4g fiber, 0mg cholesterol, 5mg sodium, 140mg potassium.

Soothing Spinach & Strawberry Synergy

Yield: 2 servings | Prep time: 10 minutes | Cook time: 2 minutes.
Ingredients:

- 200g spinach
- 150g strawberries
- 20ml lemon juice
- 150ml water

Directions:

1. Wash the spinach and strawberries.
2. Juice both ingredients.
3. Add lemon juice and water.
4. Stir and serve chilled.

Nutritional information (per 100g): 20 calories, 1.5g protein, 4g carbohydrates, 0.2g fat, 1.6g fiber, 0mg cholesterol, 25mg sodium, 180mg potassium.

Carrot & Cilantro Cooler

Yield: 2 servings | Prep time: 10 minutes | Cook time: 2 minutes.
Ingredients:
- 3 carrots (approx. 300g)
- 30g fresh cilantro (coriander)
- 150ml water

Directions:
1. Wash and peel the carrots.
2. Wash the cilantro.
3. Juice the carrots and cilantro.
4. Add water, mix, and serve chilled.

Nutritional information (per 100g): 25 calories, 0.8g protein, 6g carbohydrates, 0.2g fat, 1.8g fiber, 0mg cholesterol, 40mg sodium, 210mg potassium.

Turmeric Tranquility

Yield: 3 servings | Prep time: 10 minutes | Cook time: 2 minutes.
Ingredients:
- 40g turmeric root
- 2 carrots (approx. 200g)
- 1 apple (approx. 200g)
- 300ml water

Directions:
1. Grate the turmeric root.
2. Wash and chop the carrots and apple.
3. Combine all ingredients in a juicer.
4. Blend until smooth and serve.

Nutritional information (per 100g): 35 calories, 0.6g protein, 8g carbohydrates, 0.2g fat, 1.4g fiber, 0mg cholesterol, 15mg sodium, 110mg potassium.

Pineapple Peace

Yield: 4 servings | Prep time: 15 minutes | Cook time: 2 minutes.
Ingredients:
- 500g pineapple
- 2 oranges (approx. 400g)
- 30g ginger root
- 400ml water

Directions:
1. Peel and chop the pineapple and oranges.
2. Grate the ginger root.
3. Juice all ingredients.
4. Add water, blend, and serve.

Nutritional information (per 100g): 45 calories, 0.7g protein, 11g carbohydrates, 0.3g fat, 1.2g fiber, 0mg cholesterol, 10mg sodium, 130mg potassium.

Berry Bliss

Yield: 4 servings | Prep time: 10 minutes | Cook time: 2 minutes.
Ingredients:
- 200g blueberries
- 200g strawberries
- 1 apple (approx. 200g)
- 400ml water

Directions:
1. Wash and prep the fruits.
2. Juice them together.
3. Add water, blend, and serve.

Nutritional information (per 100g): 40 calories, 0.6g protein, 9g carbohydrates, 0.3g fat, 1.5g fiber, 0mg cholesterol, 5mg sodium, 85mg potassium.

Cool Cucumber Concoction

Yield: 3 servings | Prep time: 10 minutes | Cook time: 2 minutes.
Ingredients:
- 3 cucumbers (approx. 750g)
- 30g mint leaves
- 300ml water

Directions:
1. Wash and chop cucumbers.
2. Add cucumbers and mint to the juicer.
3. Blend until smooth. Mix with water and serve.

Nutritional information (per 100g): 15 calories, 0.7g protein, 3g carbohydrates, 0.2g fat, 0.8g fiber, 0mg cholesterol, 10mg sodium, 95mg potassium.

Charming Cherry Chill

Yield: 4 servings | Prep time: 15 minutes | Cook time: 2 minutes.
Ingredients:
- 500g cherries (pitted)
- 1 lemon (approx. 100g)
- 500ml water

Directions:
1. Pit the cherries.
2. Juice cherries and lemon.
3. Add water, stir, and serve.

Nutritional information (per 100g): 45 calories, 0.6g protein, 11g carbohydrates, 0.3g fat, 1.4g fiber, 0mg cholesterol, 3mg sodium, 120mg potassium.

Green Ginger Glow

Yield: 3 servings | Prep time: 10 minutes | Cook time: 2 minutes.
Ingredients:
- 200g spinach
- 1 cucumber (approx. 250g)
- 30g ginger root
- 300ml water

Directions:
1. Wash and prep spinach and cucumber.
2. Grate the ginger root.
3. Juice all ingredients.
4. Mix with water and serve.

Nutritional information (per 100g): 20 calories, 1g protein, 4g carbohydrates, 0.2g fat, 1g fiber, 0mg cholesterol, 15mg sodium, 90mg potassium.

Beetroot Breeze

Yield: 4 servings | Prep time: 10 minutes | Cook time: 2 minutes.
Ingredients:
- 4 beetroots (approx. 600g)
- 2 apples (approx. 400g)
- 500ml water

Directions:
1. Peel and chop the beetroots and apples.
2. Juice the ingredients.
3. Add water, blend, and serve.

Nutritional information (per 100g): 40 calories, 0.9g protein, 9g carbohydrates, 0.2g fat, 1.8g fiber, 0mg cholesterol, 30mg sodium, 110mg potassium.

Tangy Turmeric Twist

Yield: 2 servings | Prep time: 10 minutes | Cook time: 2 minutes.
Ingredients:
- 2 oranges (approx. 400g)
- 40g turmeric root
- 200ml water

Directions:
1. Peel and chop the oranges.
2. Grate the turmeric root.
3. Juice oranges and turmeric.
4. Mix with water and serve.

Nutritional information (per 100g): 40 calories, 0.8g protein, 9g carbohydrates, 0.3g fat, 1.2g fiber, 0mg cholesterol, 5mg sodium, 130mg potassium.

Mellow Melon Medley

Yield: 4 servings | Prep time: 15 minutes | Cook time: 2 minutes.

Ingredients:
- 1 medium watermelon (approx. 1kg without rind)
- 1 cucumber (approx. 250g)
- 500ml water

Directions:
1. Chop the watermelon and cucumber.
2. Juice the ingredients.
3. Combine with water and serve.

Nutritional information (per 100g): 25 calories, 0.6g protein, 6g carbohydrates, 0.2g fat, 0.5g fiber, 0mg cholesterol, 8mg sodium, 110mg potassium.

Carrot Calm

Yield: 4 servings | Prep time: 10 minutes | Cook time: 2 minutes.

Ingredients:
- 6 carrots (approx. 600g)
- 1 apple (approx. 200g)
- 500ml water

Directions:
1. Wash and chop the carrots and apples.
2. Juice them.
3. Add water, blend, and serve.

Nutritional information (per 100g): 35 calories, 0.8g protein, 8g carbohydrates, 0.3g fat, 1.6g fiber, 0mg cholesterol, 25mg sodium, 150mg potassium.

WEIGHT MANAGEMENT

Pear & Parsley Power

Yield: 2 servings | Prep time: 10 minutes | Cook time: 2 minutes.
Ingredients:
- 2 pears (approx. 360g)
- 30g parsley
- 150ml water

Directions:
1. Wash and core the pears. Wash the parsley.
2. Juice both ingredients.
3. Add water, mix, and serve.

Nutritional information (per 100g): 35 calories, 0.6g protein, 9g carbohydrates, 0.2g fat, 2g fiber, 0mg cholesterol, 15mg sodium, 130mg potassium.

Crisp Carrot Crush

Yield: 2 servings | Prep time: 10 minutes | Cook time: 2 minutes.
Ingredients:
- 3 carrots (approx. 300g)
- 1 celery stalk (approx. 60g)
- 20ml ginger juice
- 150ml water

Directions:
1. Wash and peel the carrots.
2. Wash the celery.
3. Juice the carrots and celery.
4. Mix with ginger juice and water.
5. Serve chilled.

Nutritional information (per 100g): 20 calories, 0.6g protein, 5g carbohydrates, 0.2g fat, 1.5g fiber, 0mg cholesterol, 35mg sodium, 210mg potassium.

Metabolism-Boosting Beet Blend

Yield: 2 servings | Prep time: 10 minutes | Cook time: 2 minutes.
Ingredients:
- 2 beetroots (approx. 300g)
- 1 apple (approx. 150g)
- 150ml water

Directions:
1. Wash, peel, and chop the beetroots.
2. Wash and core the apple.
3. Juice both ingredients.
4. Mix with water and serve immediately.

Nutritional information (per 100g): 35 calories, 0.8g protein, 8g carbohydrates, 0.3g fat, 2g fiber, 0mg cholesterol, 40mg sodium, 220mg potassium.

Chia Charge-Up

Yield: 2 servings | Prep time: 15 minutes | Cook time: 2 minutes.
Ingredients:
- 2 apples (approx. 300g)
- 30ml lemon juice
- 15g chia seeds
- 150ml water

Directions:
1. Wash and core the apples.
2. Juice the apples.
3. Mix with lemon juice, chia seeds, and water.
4. Let sit for 5 minutes for chia seeds to expand.
5. Serve immediately.

Nutritional information (per 100g): 40 calories, 1g protein, 10g carbohydrates, 0.5g fat, 2.5g fiber, 0mg cholesterol, 3mg sodium, 110mg potassium.

Lean Green Machine

Yield: 4 servings | Prep time: 10 minutes | Cook time: 2 minutes.
Ingredients:
- 300g spinach
- 4 celery stalks (approx. 400g)
- 2 cucumbers (approx. 500g)
- 500ml water

Directions:
1. Wash and chop spinach, celery, and cucumbers.
2. Juice all the vegetables together.
3. Mix with water and serve.

Nutritional information (per 100g): 15 calories, 1g protein, 3g carbohydrates, 0.1g fat, 1.2g fiber, 0mg cholesterol, 20mg sodium, 140mg potassium.

Fat Purge Combo

Yield: 3 servings | Prep time: 10 minutes | Cook time: 2 minutes.
Ingredients:
- 3 grapefruits (approx. 900g)
- 1 lemon (approx. 100g)
- 300ml water

Directions:
1. Peel and chop the grapefruits.
2. Squeeze juice from the grapefruits and lemon.
3. Combine with water and serve.

Nutritional information (per 100g): 35 calories, 0.7g protein, 8g carbohydrates, 0.2g fat, 1.4g fiber, 0mg cholesterol, 5mg sodium, 140mg potassium.

Berry Burn Boost

Yield: 3 servings | Prep time: 10 minutes | Cook time: 2 minutes.
Ingredients:
- 200g raspberries
- 200g blueberries
- 1 apple (approx. 200g)
- 300ml water

Directions:
1. Wash the fruits.
2. Juice them together.
3. Mix with water and serve.

Nutritional information (per 100g): 40 calories, 0.6g protein, 9g carbohydrates, 0.3g fat, 2g fiber, 0mg cholesterol, 5mg sodium, 75mg potassium.

Tropical Slim-Down

Yield: 4 servings | Prep time: 15 minutes | Cook time: 2 minutes.
Ingredients:
- 500g pineapple
- 2 kiwis (approx. 200g)
- 500ml water

Directions:
1. Peel and chop pineapple and kiwis.
2. Juice the fruits.
3. Add water, blend, and serve.

Nutritional information (per 100g): 35 calories, 0.6g protein, 8g carbohydrates, 0.2g fat, 1.2g fiber, 0mg cholesterol, 5mg sodium, 110mg potassium.

Pomegranate Power Potion

Yield: 3 servings | Prep time: 15 minutes | Cook time: 2 minutes.
Ingredients:
- 3 pomegranates (approx. 600g seeds)
- 1 orange (approx. 200g)
- 300ml water

Directions:
1. Extract seeds from pomegranates.
2. Peel the orange.
3. Juice pomegranate seeds and orange together.
4. Mix with water and serve.

Nutritional information (per 100g): 50 calories, 0.9g protein, 11g carbohydrates, 0.5g fat, 2g fiber, 0mg cholesterol, 5mg sodium, 130mg potassium.

Ginger Grape Grind

Yield: 3 servings | Prep time: 10 minutes | Cook time: 2 minutes.
Ingredients:
- 400g grapes
- 30g ginger root
- 300ml water

Directions:
1. Wash the grapes.
2. Grate the ginger root.
3. Juice grapes and ginger.
4. Mix with water and serve.

Nutritional information (per 100g): 40 calories, 0.6g protein, 9g carbohydrates, 0.3g fat, 0.9g fiber, 0mg cholesterol, 5mg sodium, 90mg potassium.

Aloe Apple Appetite Away

Yield: 2 servings | Prep time: 10 minutes | Cook time: 2 minutes.
Ingredients:
- 2 apples (approx. 400g)
- 100ml aloe vera juice

Directions:
1. Wash and chop the apples.
2. Juice the apples.
3. Mix apple juice with aloe vera juice and serve.

Nutritional information (per 100g): 40 calories, 0.2g protein, 10g carbohydrates, 0.2g fat, 1.8g fiber, 0mg cholesterol, 5mg sodium, 75mg potassium.

Cabbage Crush Control

Yield: 3 servings | Prep time: 10 minutes | Cook time: 2 minutes.
Ingredients:
- 300g green cabbage
- 2 apples (approx. 400g)
- 300ml water

Directions:
1. Wash and chop cabbage and apples.
2. Juice them together.
3. Mix with water and serve.

Nutritional information (per 100g): 25 calories, 0.7g protein, 6g carbohydrates, 0.2g fat, 1.5g fiber, 0mg cholesterol, 15mg sodium, 90mg potassium.

Zesty Zucchini Zoom

Yield: 4 servings | Prep time: 10 minutes | Cook time: 2 minutes.
Ingredients:
- 4 zucchinis (approx. 800g)
- 2 lemons (approx. 200g)
- 500ml water

Directions:
1. Wash and chop zucchinis.
2. Juice zucchinis and lemons.
3. Add water, stir, and serve.

Nutritional information (per 100g): 15 calories, 0.8g protein, 3g carbohydrates, 0.2g fat, 0.9g fiber, 0mg cholesterol, 10mg sodium, 120mg potassium.

Slim Sage Smoothie

Yield: 2 servings | Prep time: 5 minutes | Cook time: 2 minutes.
Ingredients:
- 40g fresh sage leaves
- 2 apples (approx. 400g)
- 200ml water

Directions:
1. Wash the sage leaves.
2. Chop the apples.
3. Juice sage and apples together.
4. Mix with water and serve.

Nutritional information (per 100g): 35 calories, 0.5g protein, 8g carbohydrates, 0.3g fat, 1.6g fiber, 0mg cholesterol, 5mg sodium, 80mg potassium.

SKIN HEALTH

Berry Repair Punch

Yield: 2 servings | Prep time: 10 minutes | Cook time: 2 minutes.
Ingredients:
- 150g strawberries
- 100g blueberries
- 100g raspberries
- 100ml water

Directions:
1. Wash all the berries thoroughly.
2. Juice them together.
3. Add water to achieve your preferred consistency.
4. Mix well and serve chilled.

Nutritional information (per 100g): 30 calories, 0.7g protein, 7g carbohydrates, 0.3g fat, 2g fiber, 0mg cholesterol, 1mg sodium, 90mg potassium.

Beta-Carotene Boost

Yield: 3 servings | Prep time: 15 minutes | Cook time: 2 minutes.
Ingredients:
- 300g carrots
- 1 orange (approx. 130g)
- 1 small piece of ginger (10g)
- 150ml water

Directions:
1. Wash and peel the carrots.
2. Juice the carrots, orange, and ginger.
3. Add water to get the desired consistency.
4. Stir well and serve chilled.

Nutritional information (per 100g): 28 calories, 0.6g protein, 6.5g carbohydrates, 0.1g fat, 1.2g fiber, 0mg cholesterol, 30mg sodium, 150mg potassium.

Brightening Beet & Berry Boost

Yield: 2 servings | Prep time: 10 minutes | Cook time: 2 minutes.
Ingredients:
- 1 beetroot (approx. 150g)
- 150g mixed berries (blueberries, raspberries)
- 150ml water

Directions:
1. Wash and chop the beetroot and berries.
2. Juice all ingredients.
3. Add water, mix, and serve.

Nutritional information (per 100g): 30 calories, 0.9g protein, 7g carbohydrates, 0.2g fat, 2g fiber, 0mg cholesterol, 20mg sodium, 140mg potassium.

Tropical Skin Soothe

Yield: 2 servings | Prep time: 10 minutes | Cook time: 2 minutes.
Ingredients:
- 250g pineapple
- 100g papaya
- 20ml lime juice
- 100ml coconut water

Directions:
1. Prepare the pineapple and papaya by removing the skin and seeds.
2. Juice both fruits.
3. Mix in the lime juice and coconut water.
4. Stir well and serve immediately.

Nutritional information (per 100g): 35 calories, 0.3g protein, 8.5g carbohydrates, 0.1g fat, 0.9g fiber, 0mg cholesterol, 10mg sodium, 110mg potassium.

Glowing Green Elixir

Yield: 2 servings | Prep time: 10 minutes | Cook time: 2 minutes.
Ingredients:
- 200g spinach
- 2 medium-sized cucumbers (approx. 300g)
- 1 green apple (approx. 150g)
- 20ml lemon juice
- 100ml water

Directions:
1. Wash and prepare all the ingredients.
2. Juice the spinach, cucumbers, and green apple.
3. Mix in the lemon juice.
4. Add water to get the desired consistency.
5. Stir well and serve.

Nutritional information (per 100g): 20 calories, 0.8g protein, 4g carbohydrates, 0.2g fat, 0.7g fiber, 0mg cholesterol, 10mg sodium, 90mg potassium.

Golden Glow Turmeric Tonic

Yield: 2 servings | Prep time: 10 minutes | Cook time: 2 minutes.
Ingredients:
- 20g fresh turmeric root
- 1 carrot (approx. 100g)
- 1 orange (approx. 130g)
- 100ml water

Directions:
1. Peel the turmeric root and carrot.
2. Juice the turmeric, carrot, and orange together.
3. Add water to adjust consistency.
4. Stir well and serve immediately.

Nutritional information (per 100g): 25 calories, 0.6g protein, 6g carbohydrates, 0.2g fat, 1.3g fiber, 0mg cholesterol, 20mg sodium, 120mg potassium.

Aloe Vera Hydrator

Yield: 2 servings | Prep time: 15 minutes | Cook time: 2 minutes.
Ingredients:
- 100ml aloe vera juice (preferably fresh)
- 1 cucumber (approx. 150g)
- 1 green apple (approx. 150g)
- 100ml water

Directions:
1. Prepare the cucumber and green apple.
2. Juice both ingredients.
3. Combine with the aloe vera juice.
4. Add water to adjust consistency.
5. Stir well and serve.

Nutritional information (per 100g): 20 calories, 0.5g protein, 4.8g carbohydrates, 0.1g fat, 0.6g fiber, 0mg cholesterol, 10mg sodium, 75mg potassium.

Kale Skin Repair

Yield: 2 servings | Prep time: 10 minutes | Cook time: 2 minutes.
Ingredients:
- 200g kale
- 1 pear (approx. 180g)
- 20ml lemon juice
- 100ml water

Directions:
1. Wash the kale and pear thoroughly.
2. Remove the seeds from the pear.
3. Juice both the kale and pear together.
4. Mix in the lemon juice.
5. Add water to achieve your preferred consistency.
6. Stir well and serve immediately.

Nutritional information (per 100g): 32 calories, 1.2g protein, 7g carbohydrates, 0.3g fat, 1.5g fiber, 0mg cholesterol, 25mg sodium, 125mg potassium.

Radiant Red Cabbage Magic

Yield: 4 servings | Prep time: 15 minutes | Cook time: 2 minutes.
Ingredients:
- 250g red cabbage
- 2 oranges (approx. 260g)
- 1 apple (approx. 150g)
- 150ml water

Directions:
1. Wash the red cabbage, oranges, and apple.
2. Juice them all together.
3. Add water to reach the desired consistency, mix well and serve.

Nutritional information (per 100g): 30 calories, 0.8g protein, 7g carbohydrates, 0.2g fat, 1.2g fiber, 0mg cholesterol, 20mg sodium, 130mg potassium.

Omega Radiance

Yield: 3 servings | Prep time: 15 minutes | Cook time: 2 minutes.
Ingredients:
- 150g flax seeds
- 250g mango
- 1 orange (approx. 130g)
- 150ml water

Directions:
1. Soak flax seeds in water for 10 minutes to release the gel-like substance.
2. Peel and pit the mango and orange.
3. Juice the mango and orange.
4. Blend the juice with the soaked flax seeds using a blender.
5. Add water to achieve the desired consistency.
6. Stir well and serve.

Nutritional information (per 100g): 60 calories, 1.8g protein, 9g carbohydrates, 2.5g fat, 2.8g fiber, 0mg cholesterol, 10mg sodium, 140mg potassium.

Cleansing Celery Blend

Yield: 2 servings | Prep time: 10 minutes | Cook time: 2 minutes.
Ingredients:
- 250g celery stalks
- 1 apple (approx. 150g)
- 15ml lemon juice
- 100ml water

Directions:
1. Wash the celery and apple thoroughly.
2. Juice the celery and apple together.
3. Mix in the lemon juice.
4. Add water to get the desired consistency, stir well and serve chilled.

Nutritional information (per 100g): 18 calories, 0.5g protein, 4g carbohydrates, 0.2g fat, 1.2g fiber, 0mg cholesterol, 40mg sodium, 105mg potassium.

Luscious Lemon Mint Refresher

Yield: 4 servings | Prep time: 10 minutes | Cook time: 2 minutes.
Ingredients:
- 30ml lemon juice
- 150g cucumber
- 30g fresh mint leaves
- 200ml water

Directions:
1. Wash the cucumber and mint leaves.
2. Juice the cucumber and mint leaves together.
3. Mix in the lemon juice.
4. Add water to achieve your preferred consistency, stir well and serve chilled.

Nutritional information (per 100g): 10 calories, 0.4g protein, 2.5g carbohydrates, 0.1g fat, 0.7g fiber, 0mg cholesterol, 8mg sodium, 60mg potassium.

Beet Beauty Burst

Yield: 3 servings | Prep time: 15 minutes | Cook time: 2 minutes.

Ingredients:
- 200g beetroot
- 150g red grapes
- 1 apple (approx. 150g)
- 150ml water

Directions:
1. Wash and peel the beetroot.
2. Wash the red grapes and apple.
3. Juice the beetroot, grapes, and apple together.
4. Add water to get the desired consistency.
5. Stir well and serve chilled.

Nutritional information (per 100g): 35 calories, 0.7g protein, 8g carbohydrates, 0.2g fat, 1.4g fiber, 0mg cholesterol, 30mg sodium, 110mg potassium.

Soothing Spinach Soother

Yield: 2 servings | Prep time: 10 minutes | Cook time: 2 minutes.

Ingredients:
- 250g spinach
- 1 kiwi (approx. 100g)
- 20ml lime juice
- 100ml water

Directions:
1. Wash the spinach and kiwi.
2. Peel the kiwi.
3. Juice the spinach and kiwi together.
4. Add lime juice and water, mix well and serve.

Nutritional information (per 100g): 25 calories, 1.5g protein, 5g carbohydrates, 0.3g fat, 1.6g fiber, 0mg cholesterol, 20mg sodium, 190mg potassium.

Broccoli Brilliance

Yield: 2 servings | Prep time: 15 minutes | Cook time: 2 minutes.

Ingredients:
- 200g broccoli
- 1 pear (approx. 180g)
- 1 lemon (approx. 60g, juiced)
- 100ml water

Directions:
1. Wash the broccoli and pear.
2. Juice the broccoli and pear together.
3. Add fresh lemon juice.
4. Mix with water to reach the desired consistency.
5. Stir and serve.

Nutritional information (per 100g): 28 calories, 1.1g protein, 6g carbohydrates, 0.3g fat, 1.5g fiber, 0mg cholesterol, 20mg sodium, 130mg potassium.

Tomato & Basil Beauty Tonic

Yield: 2 servings | Prep time: 10 minutes | Cook time: 2 minutes.

Ingredients:

- 3 tomatoes (approx. 300g)
- 20g fresh basil leaves
- 150ml water

Directions:

1. Wash and chop the tomatoes. Wash the basil leaves.
2. Juice both ingredients.
3. Add water, mix, and serve chilled.

Nutritional information (per 100g): 20 calories, 0.9g protein, 4.5g carbohydrates, 0.2g fat, 1.2g fiber, 0mg cholesterol, 5mg sodium, 220mg potassium.

DIABETIC FRIENDLY

Refreshing Zucchini Zen

Yield: 2 servings | Prep time: 10 minutes | Cook time: 2 minutes.
Ingredients:
- 200g zucchini
- 100g green bell pepper

Directions:
1. Wash and chop the zucchini and bell pepper.
2. Juice both ingredients.
3. Serve chilled.

Nutritional information (per 100g): 17 calories, 1.1g protein, 3.6g carbohydrates, 0.2g fat, 1g fiber, 0mg cholesterol, 2mg sodium, 262mg potassium.

Broccoli Breeze

Yield: 2 servings | Prep time: 10 minutes | Cook time: 2 minutes.
Ingredients:
- 150g broccoli
- 150g cauliflower

Directions:
1. Wash the broccoli and cauliflower.
2. Chop into juicer-friendly pieces.
3. Juice the ingredients.
4. Serve immediately.

Nutritional information (per 100g): 25 calories, 2g protein, 5g carbohydrates, 0.3g fat, 2.5g fiber, 0mg cholesterol, 30mg sodium, 300mg potassium.

Tomato Tango

Yield: 2 servings | Prep time: 10 minutes | Cook time: 2 minutes.
Ingredients:
- 250g tomatoes
- 50g celery

Directions:
1. Wash the tomatoes and celery.
2. Chop into manageable pieces.
3. Juice the ingredients together.
4. Serve chilled.

Nutritional information (per 100g): 18 calories, 0.9g protein, 3.9g carbohydrates, 0.2g fat, 1.2g fiber, 0mg cholesterol, 25mg sodium, 290mg potassium.

Cabbage Calm

Yield: 2 servings | Prep time: 10 minutes | Cook time: 2 minutes.
Ingredients:
- 200g green cabbage
- 100g cucumber

Directions:
1. Wash and chop the cabbage and cucumber.
2. Juice both ingredients.
3. Serve immediately.

Nutritional information (per 100g): 22 calories, 1.3g protein, 4.8g carbohydrates, 0.2g fat, 1.8g fiber, 0mg cholesterol, 18mg sodium, 230mg potassium.

Green Bean Gleam

Yield: 2 servings | Prep time: 10 minutes | Cook time: 2 minutes.
Ingredients:
- 200g green beans
- 100g lettuce

Directions:
1. Wash and trim the green beans.
2. Wash the lettuce.
3. Juice both ingredients.
4. Serve chilled.

Nutritional information (per 100g): 20 calories, 1.5g protein, 4.5g carbohydrates, 0.1g fat, 2.1g fiber, 0mg cholesterol, 4mg sodium, 220mg potassium.

Kale Kindness

Yield: 2 servings | Prep time: 10 minutes | Cook time: 2 minutes.
Ingredients:
- 200g kale
- 100g celery

Directions:
1. Wash the kale and celery.
2. Chop into juicer-friendly pieces.
3. Juice the ingredients.
4. Serve immediately.

Nutritional information (per 100g): 28 calories, 2.5g protein, 4.7g carbohydrates, 0.5g fat, 2g fiber, 0mg cholesterol, 45mg sodium, 320mg potassium.

Peppy Pepper Potion

Yield: 2 servings | Prep time: 10 minutes | Cook time: 2 minutes.
Ingredients:
- 150g red bell pepper
- 150g cucumber

Directions:
1. Wash and chop the bell pepper and cucumber.
2. Juice both ingredients.
3. Serve chilled.

Nutritional information (per 100g): 19 calories, 1g protein, 4.3g carbohydrates, 0.2g fat, 1.3g fiber, 0mg cholesterol, 5mg sodium, 220mg potassium.

Energizing Eggplant Elixir

Yield: 2 servings | Prep time: 10 minutes | Cook time: 2 minutes.
Ingredients:
- 200g eggplant
- 100g tomatoes

Directions:
1. Wash and chop the eggplant and tomatoes.
2. Juice both ingredients.
3. Serve immediately.

Nutritional information (per 100g): 20 calories, 1g protein, 4.8g carbohydrates, 0.2g fat, 2.1g fiber, 0mg cholesterol, 3mg sodium, 230mg potassium.

Cauliflower Cloud

Yield: 2 servings | Prep time: 10 minutes | Cook time: 2 minutes.
Ingredients:
- 250g cauliflower
- 50g celery

Directions:
1. Wash and chop the cauliflower and celery.
2. Juice both ingredients.
3. Serve chilled.

Nutritional information (per 100g): 24 calories, 2g protein, 4.9g carbohydrates, 0.3g fat, 2.3g fiber, 0mg cholesterol, 28mg sodium, 290mg potassium.

Bitter Gourd Bliss

Yield: 2 servings | Prep time: 10 minutes | Cook time: 2 minutes.
Ingredients:
- 150g bitter gourd (bitter melon)
- 100g cucumber

Directions:
1. Wash and slice the bitter gourd, removing seeds.
2. Wash and chop the cucumber.
3. Juice both ingredients together.
4. Serve immediately.

Nutritional information (per 100g): 19 calories, 1g protein, 4.3g carbohydrates, 0.2g fat, 2.4g fiber, 0mg cholesterol, 8mg sodium, 296mg potassium.

Swiss Chard Charm

Yield: 2 servings | Prep time: 10 minutes | Cook time: 2 minutes.
Ingredients:
- 200g swiss chard
- 100g celery

Directions:
1. Wash and chop swiss chard and celery.
2. Juice the ingredients together.
3. Serve chilled.

Nutritional information (per 100g): 20 calories, 1.8g protein, 3.9g carbohydrates, 0.2g fat, 1.6g fiber, 0mg cholesterol, 32mg sodium, 330mg potassium.

Brussel Burst

Yield: 2 servings | Prep time: 12 minutes | Cook time: 2 minutes.
Ingredients:
- 200g brussels sprouts
- 100g green bell pepper

Directions:
1. Wash and trim brussels sprouts.
2. Wash and chop the green bell pepper.
3. Juice both ingredients.
4. Serve immediately.

Nutritional information (per 100g): 35 calories, 2.6g protein, 6.7g carbohydrates, 0.3g fat, 3.3g fiber, 0mg cholesterol, 25mg sodium, 394mg potassium.

Collard Green Cleanse

Yield: 2 servings | Prep time: 10 minutes | Cook time: 2 minutes.
Ingredients:
- 250g collard greens
- 50g cucumber

Directions:
1. Wash and chop the collard greens and cucumber.
2. Juice the ingredients.
3. Serve immediately.

Nutritional information (per 100g): 24 calories, 2.5g protein, 4.4g carbohydrates, 0.4g fat, 3.6g fiber, 0mg cholesterol, 15mg sodium, 203mg potassium.

Radish Revive

Yield: 2 servings | Prep time: 10 minutes | Cook time: 2 minutes.
Ingredients:
- 150g radish
- 100g celery

Directions:
1. Wash and chop radish and celery.
2. Juice the ingredients together.
3. Serve chilled.

Nutritional information (per 100g): 17 calories, 0.9g protein, 3.8g carbohydrates, 0.1g fat, 1.9g fiber, 0mg cholesterol, 30mg sodium, 270mg potassium.

Turnip Twist

Yield: 2 servings | Prep time: 10 minutes | Cook time: 2 minutes.
Ingredients:
- 250g turnip
- 50g spinach

Directions:
1. Wash and chop turnips and spinach.
2. Juice the ingredients.
3. Serve immediately.

Nutritional information (per 100g): 24 calories, 1.3g protein, 5.5g carbohydrates, 0.2g fat, 1.8g fiber, 0mg cholesterol, 58mg sodium, 233mg potassium.

Dandelion Delight

Yield: 2 servings | Prep time: 10 minutes | Cook time: 2 minutes.
Ingredients:
- 200g dandelion greens
- 100g cucumber

Directions:
1. Wash and chop dandelion greens and cucumber.
2. Juice the ingredients together.
3. Serve immediately.

Nutritional information (per 100g): 27 calories, 2.7g protein, 5.1g carbohydrates, 0.6g fat, 3.5g fiber, 0mg cholesterol, 42mg sodium, 328mg potassium.

Lettuce Love

Yield: 2 servings | Prep time: 10 minutes | Cook time: 2 minutes.
Ingredients:
- 200g romaine lettuce
- 100g green bell pepper

Directions:
1. Wash and chop romaine lettuce and green bell pepper.
2. Juice the ingredients.
3. Serve chilled.

Nutritional information (per 100g): 16 calories, 1.2g protein, 3.2g carbohydrates, 0.3g fat, 2.1g fiber, 0mg cholesterol, 8mg sodium, 238mg potassium.

Green Powerhouse Juice

Yield: 2 servings | Prep time: 10 minutes | Cook time: 2 minutes.
Ingredients:
- 200g broccoli
- 50g celery

Directions:
1. Wash and chop broccoli and celery.
2. Juice both ingredients together.
3. Serve immediately.

Nutritional information (per 100g): 30 calories, 2.8g protein, 5.9g carbohydrates, 0.4g fat, 2.6g fiber, 0mg cholesterol, 33mg sodium, 316mg potassium.

Zesty Zucchini Zip

Yield: 2 servings | Prep time: 10 minutes | Cook time: 2 minutes.
Ingredients:
- 200g zucchini
- 50g green bell pepper

Directions:
1. Wash and chop zucchini and green bell pepper.
2. Juice the ingredients together.
3. Serve chilled.

Nutritional information (per 100g): 18 calories, 1.4g protein, 3.4g carbohydrates, 0.3g fat, 1.2g fiber, 0mg cholesterol, 8mg sodium, 262mg potassium.

Cabbage Boost

Yield: 2 servings | Prep time: 10 minutes | Cook time: 2 minutes.
Ingredients:
- 200g green cabbage
- 100g green beans

Directions:
1. Wash and chop the cabbage into manageable pieces.
2. Wash and trim the ends of the green beans.
3. Place cabbage and green beans into the juicer.
4. Juice the ingredients together.
5. Pour into glasses and serve immediately.

Nutritional information (per 100g): 28 calories, 1.9g protein, 5.7g carbohydrates, 0.3g fat, 2.5g fiber, 0mg cholesterol, 15mg sodium, 230mg potassium.

Note: Always monitor blood sugar levels when trying new foods or making significant dietary changes, especially for individuals with diabetes.

UNDERSTANDING RATIOS AND CREATING YOUR RECIPES JUICING

Pareto's Rule: How Does It Work in Juicing?

Pareto's principle, commonly known as the 80/20 rule, suggests that 80% of outcomes result from 20% of the causes. Initially associated with economics, this principle is used in various fields to optimize productivity and results. In the context of juicing, Pareto's Rule can be applied in numerous ways to help beginners get the most out of their juicing experience. Here's how:

1. **80% Vegetables, 20% Fruits:**
   When starting on a juicing journey, it's essential to strike a balance between taste and nutrition. A general guideline is to make juices comprising 80% vegetables and 20% fruits. Or drink one glass of juice in the morning made entirely from fruits. The rest of the juices during the day drink only vegetable ones. This ensures you get the vital nutrients from vegetables without the excess sugar from fruits. The result? A delicious, balanced juice that's beneficial for your health.

2. **Maximizing Nutrition:**
   You don't need to juice various ingredients for the most nutritional benefits. By selecting a few nutrient-dense ingredients (20%), you can derive 80% of the potential health benefits. Examples include kale, spinach, beets, and celery, all of which pack a nutritional punch.

3. **Efficiency in Preparation:**
   Instead of spending time preparing a wide assortment of fruits and vegetables, focus on a select few (20%) that provide the maximum yield (80%). For instance, cucumbers and oranges yield more juice compared to their size and weight than some other produce.

4. **Cleaning and Maintenance:**
   When it comes to maintaining your juicer, the small habits (20%) lead to the most significant outcomes (80%). For instance, rinsing your juicer parts immediately after use can prevent staining and simplify cleaning, ensuring longevity and consistent performance.

5. **Investment in Quality:**
   When buying a juicer, focus on quality, not quantity. Investing in a high-quality machine (representing the critical 20%) will ensure you extract the maximum amount of juice (the 80% outcome) from your produce, saving money in the long run.

6. **Mastering Key Recipes:**
   As a beginner, you don't need to know dozens of juice recipes. Focus on mastering a few (20%) that deliver the desired taste and health benefits. These staple recipes can be your go-to options, ensuring you enjoy 80% of your juicing experiences.

In essence, Pareto's Principle is all about efficiency. Applying this 80/20 rule to your juicing habits allows you to optimize the time, money, and effort you invest while enjoying the myriad benefits of fresh, homemade juice

PROPER INTRODUCTION OF JUICES INTO YOUR DIET

Starting a juicing journey can be exciting, promising a world of nutritional benefits and an array of vibrant flavors. However, like any significant dietary change, incorporating juices should be gradual, thoughtful, and strategic to ensure the body adapts positively. Here are the steps and considerations for a smooth transition:

Before introducing juices into your diet, consult with your doctor and nutritionist. If necessary, get some tests done: a complete blood count and an allergy test. This way, you will minimize the risks of adverse effects on your body and will be able to choose the products and recipes that will benefit you only.

1. **Start Small:**
   As with any dietary change, starting slow is always a good idea. Begin by introducing small amounts of juice (around 4-6 oz) a few times a week. This will allow your digestive system to acclimate to the liquid nutrition. But don't overuse sweet juices - the daily intake in its pure form should be at most 150 ml.

2. **Go Green Gradually:**
   Green juices, made primarily from green vegetables, can be potent and might have a strong flavor that some beginners find challenging. Start by making juices that mix fruits and a small amount of greens. As your palate adjusts, you can increase the amount of greens.

3. **Listen to Your Body:**
   Everyone's body is different. Pay attention to how your body reacts to certain juices. Consider modifying the ingredients or quantity if a particular mix causes digestive discomfort or other adverse reactions.

4. **Balancing Act:**
   While juices offer numerous vitamins and minerals, they lack other essential nutrients like protein and fat. Ensure you're still consuming a balanced diet. Juices should complement your meals, only replace them partially.

5. **Quality Over Quantity:**
   Opt for organic produce whenever possible to reduce the ingestion of pesticides and other chemicals. Fresh, high-quality fruits and vegetables will yield better nutritional value.

6. **Hydration is Key:**
   While juices contribute to your daily fluid intake, they don't replace the need for plain water. Ensure you stay hydrated throughout the day, especially if you consume more diuretic juices like those made from cucumber or watermelon.

7. **Mindful of Sugars:**
   Fruits are naturally high in sugars. To avoid too much sugar, mix fruit juices with vegetable juices. Vegetables like cucumber, celery, and carrots can provide a mild flavor without added sugars.

8. **Transitioning Period:**
   As you integrate more juices into your diet, you might experience detoxification symptoms, such as headaches or changes in bowel movement. These symptoms are typically temporary, but always consult a healthcare professional if you're concerned.

30-DAY MEEL PLAN TO LOSE WEIGHT

Day 1

Breakfast: Green Power Juice:
Ingredients: 100g kale, 100g spinach, 150g cucumber, 2 green apples (approx. 300g), 30ml lemon juice (juice from about 1 lemon). Nutritional information (per 100g): calories: 31, protein: 0.9g, carbohydrates: 7.3g, fat: 0.2g, fiber: 1.4g
Lunch: Grilled chicken salad with olive oil dressing.
Dinner: Vegetable stir-fry with tofu.

Day 2

Breakfast: Berry Boost Juice: 200g strawberries,150g blueberries, 150g raspberries, 1 large apple (approximately 200g).
Nutritional information (per 100g):calories: 50, protein: 0.5g, carbohydrates: 12g, fat: 0.3g, fiber: 2.5g.
Lunch: Lentil soup with whole grain bread
Dinner: Baked salmon with steamed broccoli

Day 3

Breakfast: Tropical Delight Juice: 150g pineapple, 100g mango, 100ml orange juice (freshly squeezed from about 2 oranges).
Nutritional Information (per 100g): calories: 50 kcal, protein: 0.6g, carbohydrates: 12.5g, fat: 0.2g, fiber: 1.2g.
Lunch: Turkey wrap with lettuce, tomato, and light mayo
Dinner: Chicken with steamed green beans

Day 4

Breakfast: Detox Juice: 100g beetroot, 100g carrot, 10g ginger, 100g apple, 100 ml water (to adjust consistency if needed).
Nutritional Information (per 100g): calories: 45 kcal, protein: 0.8g, carbohydrates: 10.5g, fat: 0.2g, fiber: 2.2g.
Lunch: Quinoa salad with roasted veggies and feta
Dinner: Grilled steak with asparagus and side salad

Day 5

Breakfast: Citrus Burst Juice: 150g orange, 150g grapefruit, 50g lemon, 50ml Cold water (optional, for desired consistency).

Nutritional information (per 100g): calories: 40 kcal, protein: 0.7g, carbohydrates: 9.3g, fat: 0.2g, fiber: 1.2g.
Lunch: Tuna salad with mixed greens
Dinner: Stir-fry with lean beef, bell peppers, and snap peas

Day 6

Breakfast: Antioxidant Juice: 100g pomegranate (seeds), 100g blueberries, 10g assai puree or powder, 50ml cold water (optional, to adjust consistency).
Nutritional information (per 100g): calories: 70 kcal, protein: 0.8g, carbohydrates: 15.6g, fat: 0.7g, fiber: 2.8g.
Lunch: Chicken Caesar salad (light dressing)
Dinner: Baked cod with quinoa and sautéed spinach

Day 7

Breakfast: Rejuvenate Juice: 100h celery, 100g cucumber, 10g fresh mint leaves, 50g lime (approximately the juice of one medium lime), 50ml cold water (optional, for desired consistency)
Nutritional information (per 100g): calories: 10 kcal, protein: 0.5g, carbohydrates: 2.2g, fat: 0.1g, fiber: 0.8g.
Lunch: Whole grain wrap with hummus, sprouts, and veggies
Dinner: Lemon herb roasted chicken with Brussels sprouts

Day 8

Breakfast: Skin Glow Juice: 100g carrot, 100g apple, 100g orange.
Nutritional information (per 100g): calories: 41 kcal, protein: 0.6g, carbohydrates: 10g, fat: 0.2g, fiber: 2.2g.
Lunch: Spinach and feta stuffed chicken breast with side salad
Dinner: Vegetarian curry with brown rice

Day 9

Breakfast: Refreshing Melon Juice: 150g watermelon, 150g honeydew, 50g lime (approximately the juice of one medium lime)
Nutritional information (per 100g): calories: 28 kcal, protein: 0.5g, carbohydrates: 7g, fat: 0.1g, fiber: 0.6g.
Lunch: Avocado and egg salad on whole-grain toast
Dinner: Teriyaki grilled chicken with bok choy and broccoli

Day 10

Breakfast: Red Vitality Juice: 150g tomato, 100g red bell pepper, 50g carrot, 50g celery.
Nutritional information (per 100g): calories: 20 kcal, protein: 0.8g, carbohydrates: 4.5g, fat: 0.2g, fiber: 1.4g.
Lunch: Spinach, goat cheese, and beet salad with walnuts
Dinner: Vegetable paella with saffron and lemon

Day 11

Breakfast: Energizer Juice: 150g pineapple, 100g kiwi, 50g spinach, 10g chia seeds, 50ml cold water (optional, for desired consistency).
Nutritional information (per 100g): calories: 56 kcal, protein: 1.2g, carbohydrates: 12g, fat: 0.7g, fiber: 2.5g.
Lunch: Grilled turkey and cheese sandwich with a side of vegetable soup
Dinner: Chili lime tilapia with green beans and quinoa

Day 12

Breakfast: Purple Power Juice: 100g blueberries, 100g blackberries, 100g apple, 10g chia seeds, 50ml cold water (optional, for desired consistency).
Nutritional information (per 100g): calories: 54 kcal, protein: 1.3g, carbohydrates: 12g, fat: 0.7g, fiber: 3g.
Lunch: Greek salad with olives, feta, cucumber, and cherry tomatoes
Dinner: Beef stir-fry with snap peas, carrots, and broccoli on brown rice

Day 13

Breakfast: Immunity Boost Juice: 150g orange, 150g grapefruit, 15g ginger, 5g turmeric (or a small piece roughly the size of a thumb's tip).
Nutritional information (per 100g): calories: 42 kcal, protein: 0.9g, carbohydrates: 10.3g, fat: 0.2g, fiber: 1.8g.
Lunch: Tuna and white bean salad with parsley and lemon
Dinner: Chicken fajitas with bell peppers, onions, and whole-grain tortillas

Day 14

Breakfast: Digestive Bliss Juice: 150g papaya, 100g pineapple, 10g fresh mint leaves, 5g fennel seeds (or use a small piece of fresh fennel bulb, around 30g).
Nutritional information (per 100g): calories: 38 kcal, protein: 0.6g, carbohydrates: 9.4g, fat: 0.3g, fiber: 1.5g.
Lunch: Roasted chickpea salad with tahini dressing
Dinner: Herb-crusted baked salmon with roasted zucchini and tomatoes

Day 15

Breakfast: Cleanse & Detox Juice: 150g celery, 100g kale, 50g lemon (around half a lemon), 10g ginger.
Nutritional information (per 100g): calories: 21 kcal, protein: 1.5g, carbohydrates: 4.2g, fat: 0.2g, fiber: 1.7g.
Lunch: Spinach and mushroom omelet with salsa
Dinner: Herb-crusted baked salmon with roasted zucchini and tomatoes

Repeat similar patterns with a mix of the listed juices and various healthy meals for the following weeks, ensuring a balance of nutrients, colors, and flavors. Also, remember that for a weight loss regimen, you must be in a caloric deficit, meaning you consume fewer calories than you burn. Adjust portion sizes to your needs, and add physical activity to enhance results.

WEEKLY MEEL PLAN

	BREAKFAST	LUNCH	DINNER
MON			
TUE			
WED			
THU			
FRI			
SAT			
SUN			

CONCLUSION

As we close this refreshing journey through the world of juicing, it's evident that the vibrant realm of fresh juices offers more than just tantalizing flavors; it's a gateway to health, vitality, and a deeper connection with nature's bounty. Whether sipping on a classic carrot-orange blend or venturing into exotic combinations, juicing provides an opportunity to nourish your body with essential nutrients in the most natural form.

For beginners, the initial steps into juicing can seem overwhelming with the myriad of choices in produce, equipment, and techniques. Yet, as you've discovered throughout this guide, the essence of juicing is simplicity and creativity. Embrace the journey of exploration, experimentation, and, most importantly, enjoyment. The benefits you'll reap are physical but also mental and emotional, as you'll find solace in this therapeutic activity.

Remember the core principles we've discussed as you continue your juicing adventure beyond this book. Prioritize freshness, be adventurous in your combinations, and always listen to your body's responses. The world of juicing is vast and diverse, and this book is just the starting point. Your blender and juicer are transformation tools, turning simple fruits and vegetables into liquid gold for your health.

So, here's to a healthier, more vibrant you, one glass at a time. Cheers to your juicing journey!

Made in United States
Orlando, FL
02 November 2023

38528743R00050